NFT

A Complete Guide for Beginners to Invest and Make Profit From Nfts

(The Ultimate Guide to Understand Non-fungible Tokens)

Richard Brown

Published By Richard Brown

Richard Brown

All Rights Reserved

Nft: A Complete Guide for Beginners to Invest and Make Profit From Nfts (The Ultimate Guide to Understand Non-fungible Tokens)

ISBN 978-1-77485-392-4

Legal & Disclaimer

The information contained in this book is not designed to replace or take the place of any form of medicine or professional medical advice. The information in this book has been provided for educational and entertainment purposes only.

The information contained in this book has been compiled from sources deemed reliable, and it is accurate to the best of the Author's knowledge; however, the Author cannot guarantee its accuracy and validity and cannot be held liable for any errors or omissions. Changes are periodically made to this book. You must consult your doctor or get professional medical advice before using any of the suggested remedies, techniques, or information in this book.

Upon using the information contained in this book, you agree to hold harmless the Author from and against any damages, costs, and expenses, including any legal fees potentially resulting from the application of any of the information provided by this guide. This disclaimer applies to any damages or injury caused by the use and application, whether directly or indirectly, of any advice or information presented, whether for breach of contract, tort, negligence, personal injury, criminal intent, or under any other cause of action.

You agree to accept all risks of using the information presented inside this book. You need to consult a professional medical practitioner in order to ensure you are both able and healthy enough to participate in this program.

TABLE OF CONTENTS

Introduction

Music, art, games, products, and films are just a few types of digital asset that are a reflection of the real world, such as NFTs. Most of them can be bought and sold on the internet, usually as part of a cryptocurrency exchange and are typically developed using the same software as other digital currencies.

But it is true that, even though they've been around since 2014 NFTs are gaining popularity because of the fact that they're becoming an increasingly popular means of buying and selling digital art. From November 2017 to the present, $174 million was invested in NFTs which is an all-time record.

In addition, NFTs are usually unique or at most, one of a limited supply, and only unique identification codes are used to identify them. As per Arry Yu, the head of the Washington Technology Industry Association Cascadia Blockchain Council and the managing director at Yellow

Umbrella Ventures, "in the end, NFTs create an issue of digital scarceness."

This is in stark contrast to the majority of digital media which are available in unlimited quantities. Therefore, if an product is highly sought-after cutting off the availability of the asset will increase the value of the asset.

In real life, a lot of NFTs are digital works that are already available in various forms in other locations, like famous videos from NBA games, or securitized versions of digital artwork that are being circulated on Instagram at the very least, in their initial stages.

An internationally renowned digital artist also called "Beeple," created "EVERYDAYS The First 5000 days" made up from 5,000 drawings daily which was an extremely expensive NFT ever offered by Christie's for a record $69.3 million in 2011.

On the internet, anyone can view individual photos--or even the entire collection of images for free anytime. In the end, people are willing to shell out millions of dollars for things they can capture or download at no cost.

As a non-financial purchase allows the buyer to maintain the ownership of the item. It's not just that, it also incorporates authentication that acts as a way to establish proof of ownership. It's equal to the value of the object the item itself for collectors to be able to claim these "digital pride rights."

What is the difference between an NFT and Cryptocurrency? from Cryptocurrency?

NFT stands that means non-fungible token. In general, it is developed using the same type of software as cryptocurrency like Bitcoin or Ethereum however that's about the point where they share a lot of similarities cease.

The currencies in the form of physical money and cryptocurrency have the same meaning. They are "fungible," meaning they can be exchanged or traded against one another. They're similar in regards to worth: one dollar will always equal more dollars, and a Bitcoin will always be worth another Bitcoin and the list goes on. Due to the fungibility of crypto currencies it's a secure way to finish transactions through the blockchain.

NFTs however are distinct. Each NFT is secured by a digital signature making it impossible to use them exchanged to or compared with other or in any other way (hence they are non-fungible). For instance, an NBA Top Shot clip is not comparable to every day just because they're both first-time attempts. It's important to remember the fact that the one NBA Top Shot footage is not always the same as an other NBA Top Shot clip, however.

Chapter 1: Non-Fungible Tokens

What is the meaning of Non-Fungible?

Non-Fungibility is the characteristic of a good or commodity, whose units are considered to be unique. An NFT is a Non-Fungible Coin. (NFT) can be described as a cryptocurrency token with this property.

Also, if we consider it from the perspective that of real life, it's similar to having a stake in the form of silver or gold. These shares aren't in any way fungible, and they are exclusive because they represent an asset. Therefore, if I own one percent of an ounce gold, I have only 1% of the gold bar. But, I am not able to exchange my 1% for another's 1% of the identical gold bar.

The key point lies in the fact that NFTs are unique and can not be replicated.

What is the reason we require Non-Fungible Tokens?

Imagine a scenario where you own a non-fungible token representing a car. Let's say, an Aston Martin DB9. You've put in hours and dollars collecting the token and used it to purchase services. But, the owner of Aston Martin has also used the token to purchase parts for his car. Aston Martin has used the same token to purchase parts for his vehicle. What will happen if you choose to dispose of your token? It's no longer valid since it was utilized for two different purposes This means that you won't receive the amount you could have received in the event that it were still valid.

This is among the problems which can be resolved making use of NFTs because they are unique and can't be duplicated. When they are transferred or sold the unit cannot be used by another platform as each unit is distinct. The owner is able to utilize it in any way that he likes in the time the unit is his own; however, when he transfers it to another person the owner forfeits all rights to it.

Non-fungible tokens are unique digital assets. They cannot be divided and possess distinct properties which make them an attractive digital asset.

The goal of the fungible token is that it can be exchangeable to other types of tokens.

They are used as a means of payment which can be transferred between individuals.

Non-fungible Token (NFT) can be described as a kind of token that is distinct. It isn't interchangeable. It can be distinctive due to their combination property like the name of its owner, picture as well as information about its owner. It could also be unique due to its worth.

A high-quality illustration is a collectible card. As an example for instance, if I have an autographed card from Michael Jordan and you have an identical card to Michael Jordan, there is no way for us to swap our cards. The information on the card like the number, the picture as well as names of player are exclusive.

It is also unique as it is a certain value. Cards that are collectible have an assigned value. The most expensive Michael Jordan card Michael Jordan has an assigned value that is more than the average card of Michael Jordan.

NFTs are also unique as they represent assets. They may represent ownership of land, a structure as well as a car or any other physical or digital asset. If you own an asset, it is possible to assign it a unique identification. You can provide it with an unique identification number by connecting it to the blockchain.

The possibility exists to create an asset registry that is digital using blockchain as the central registry for all assets. This is possible by using NFTs.The features of an NFT can be utilized to create a distinct. Combining these attributes makes an NFT distinctive.

Additionally, it is possible to utilize the blockchain to generate an unique identifier which links physically-based assets with the blockchain. When you connect the physical assets to the blockchain you can make electronic representations of the assets. This allows you to utilize NFTs as a representation of these properties.

Utilizing the NFTs as a way to identify physical asset makes it feasible for businesses and individuals to make use of blockchain technology. If you're looking to purchase the house of your dreams, you can keep the information regarding the property in an online asset registry and then use NFTs as unique identifiers of the property.

This way, in the event that you wish to sell the home, you can transfer ownership of the NFT to a different person. The new owner will have ownership of that particular NFT and will retain total control over that NFT. They may transfer it back or sell it via an exchange.

What is an Fungible Token?

Fungibility is the characteristic of a good or product whose components are interchangeable. It's also known as "fungible products" also known as "fungible assets". For instance, if I own a gold-plated bar and I want to trade it for another bar with the same dimensions and weight with no problem.

A fungible token is a token that has this characteristic. If we use the same instance as before when we have the Aston Martin

DB9 token and another person is using it to purchase certain parts for their car, this will not be a problem since it is an fungible token. Should I choose to dispose of my token, anyone can buy parts for their vehicle because they're all the same and have the identical Aston Martin DB9.

Non-Fungible Tokens vs Fungible Tokens

The distinction between non-fungible and fungible ones is how they are utilized and transferred between people. A fungible token is transferable from one individual to another and it doesn't matter who is the owner; However, with a non-fungible one when it is transferred to another person the token is no longer valid and can't be used by another person.

One good illustration of a fungible token can be Ether (ETH) it is the token that is used for Ethereum. Ethereum blockchain. It is possible to purchase and sell ETH whenever you wish and there's no issue with that since it is totally interchangeable. If you've purchased ETH from another person and then transferred it to them, you don't possess any say in what happens to it since it is available to use in any manner that the new owner wishes to utilize it.

They are unique since they are distinct and are not able to be replicated or copied as the other assets in digital form. If you have an NFT that you own, you have the entire rights to it, until when you want to move it it or trade it with another.

What's the difference from the use of tokens that are fungible?

When you purchase an fungible token, you purchase it with the purpose of using it for an alternative to currency.

For instance, if you purchase for instance, if you purchase Bitcoin then you can use it to purchase products or services. If you have one BTC and you have 1 BTC, it doesn't matter if the BTC comes taken from the wallet you are using, or an alternative wallet. It is still possible to make use of it to purchase items or services.

If you have an NFT like one from Michael Jordan, you do not want to offer it to another person as the person is not allowed to use the specific NFT. It's useless to them since they don't possess the card. They'll only have an unique identifier which represents the ownership of the card.

Many developers use non-fungible tokens in their applications due to the fact that they are digital assets as well as physical assets. This makes them useful digital assets that are utilized by both individuals and businesses regularly. They are utilized in games like CryptoKitties or Rarebits. Also, you can build smart contracts using non-fungible tokens like land registry records, or event tickets. Blockchain technology is currently being utilized by government agencies to store data regarding assets.

What is the difference between it and ERC20?

The ERC20 token standard was designed to make intangible tokens. This means that each token is exactly like the other token. The properties of tokens are the same and the worth of the tokens is the same.

The properties of ERC20 tokens can only be seen on the Ethereum blockchain. The Ethereum blockchain is able to determine the amount of tokens that exist and the amount they're worth.

With NFTs, it's possible to create unique identifiers to indicate ownership of an physical or digital asset. These identifiers are stored on the blockchain. Blockchains will contain the information regarding the unique identifiers, and it is possible to examine the ledger on a public database.

This allows companies and individuals to employ NFTs to enhance their applications since they can transfer the ownership of these assets one person to another without the use of intermediaries like banks or other third-party. This helps reduce expenses and makes it simpler for both businesses and individuals to trade digital assets , or physical assets like artwork, real estate jewelry, automobiles or any other physical item that could be digitally recorded with blockchain technology.

technology.

13

What is the difference between this and Ethereum?

The Ethereum blockchain is a smart contract platform which use fungible tokens to pay for goods or services.

If you own the ERC20 token you may use it to purchase services and goods via Ethereum. Ethereum blockchain.

It is also possible to use the Ethereum blockchain can also support ERC721 that is a standard used for non-fungible tokens.

Ethereum is the very first cryptocurrency to support smart contracts in which fungible tokens can be used to pay for products or services. Ethereum is also the first blockchain that supports smart contracts. Ethereum blockchain was also the very first to be able to support smart contracts that use non-fungible tokens. These tokens are used to create unique identifiers for the ownership of digital assets as well as physical assets.

This implies it is the case that Ethereum is the very first blockchain to support smart contracts that use fungible tokens. These tokens can be used to pay for goods or services and non-fungible tokens are used to identify unique identifiers that are used to identify the ownership of digital assets as well as physical assets.

The Fungibility Problem

This leads us to one of the major issues that cryptocurrencies face - the fungibility. That means that if you have 10 , Bitcoins (BTC) and anyone could take the 10 BTC from you and exchange them with another person for whatever they like without your being able take action. This is what makes Bitcoin less popular since you have no control over the fate of your money after they have been transferred or exchanged with another.

Fungibility is one of the issues that can be addressed using NFTs. In reality, one of the largest use cases for NFTs is the area of digital assets. Digital assets are not exclusive and can be utilized in any way you like for so long as you are the owner of them. If you purchase the digital asset, you are in complete control of the asset till you make the decision to sell it to another.

One of the major advantages of making use of NFTs as digital asset is that they are able to be traded or sold across different platforms without issues because they are unique and cannot be duplicated. They also alleviate the issue of double-spending since every unit is able to use more than one time. They cannot be copied or duplicated as other digital assets such as ERC-20 tokens.

Chapter 2: What Are Playing To Earn Games?

The business model referred to as Play-to-Earn is a recent advancement in the gaming industry. It's a strategy for business that supports the concept of an open economy that rewards players who contribute an advantage to the gaming environment through their contribution. It's likely to introduce new concepts for games and retention models to the current gaming that hasn't been ever before.

With the advancement of technology becoming more accessible to the public at large businesses for video games were developed. In the latter part of the 1970s and into the early 1980s, we would play our video games in arcades in local gaming centers. With only a quarter of a dollar in their pockets, players were competing for the top score.

Today gamers game on our smartphones while on public transport or having breaks.

We play games on our home or computer consoles when we want to experience a greater immersion. Whatever the platform the game is played on, every player can come across a plan of action that is suitable for their needs.

The base is free to play.

The consumer must purchase an access license to play the premium games. This is done by buying the license through a digital retailer or by purchasing a physical copy purchased from brick-and-mortar stores or online. The financial commitment is quite significant because it's not uncommon to pay as much as $60 for a game that is just launched. While it is an extremely popular market however, the free-to-play model has seen the highest expansion in recent years.

The business model of free-to-play allows players to play without cost. Freemium or free-to-play games are available to download at all times and offer users limited or restricted experience. Gamers are required to pay in order to speed up their progress, or obtain exclusive equipment. Players may have to purchase in-game currency as well as additional materials or specific cosmetics to their characters in game such as.

Many of the most played games available are available for free. Fortnite alone brought in 1.8 billion dollars worth of revenue last year, despite the fact that the game of battle royale is completely free. Selling cosmetics that allow for more personalization is a lucrative business. One of the most well-known games that are available include League of Legends and Hearthstone that are virtually free. Every developer has a strategy to charge players for additional materials or visuals.

These games for free have produced billions of dollars of revenue and there is absolutely nothing to suggest that that they are going to stop. This shows that the free-to-play business model is gaining traction and that game developers have learned the art of making money from free-to-play games.

The business model that is based on play-to-earn has many similarities with the model of free-to-play. A lot of times, a play-to earn game includes mechanics that are found in free-to-play games. But, they also provide the chance for players to earn money, or digital items.

Explaination of earn-while-you-play

The ability to give players ownership of game assets and the capability to increase their value through active gameplay are key elements of the model of play-to-earn. Through participation in the game's economy, players help the advancement of the game, which benefits others as well as the game's creators. They receive in-game currency in the process. These digital assets can vary from gaming assets that are tokenized via the blockchain. This is the reason the business model of play-to-earn is a great complement to blockchain games.

The model of play-to-earn reward players by rewarding their effort and time into the sport. For instance, players who play Axie Infinity get Small Love Potions (SLP). These tokens are needed by players to increase the number of Axies they breed, but they

20

also have the option of selling SLP on the open market for other gamers. Other examples include the resources through League of Kingdoms and the rewards in the fantasy football game so uncommon.

To participate, you must earn a certain amount of money.

In most cases, a pay-to win game is one that's accessible for free. However, that is not always the case. In the moment, players have to buy three Axies before they can fight in Lunacia Axie Infinity's realm. Also, it is not common to demand players to spend cash on player cards prior to getting cards from weekly tournaments. Although games such as Chainz Arena and League of Kingdoms are completely free for players to enjoy, the inefficient game mechanics and limitations force players to put some money to play the game. Therefore, even if players make a profit however, they are also required to be able to pay.

It is expensive to create games that are video-based which is produced by companies. The benefit of the business model of play-to-earn in contrast is that players is always creating something valuable that could be traded. Even if the player has to start by paying for the game, these purchased items could be sold again. Every card from So uncommon, and every Axie you have in your wallet could be offered for sale. In parallel, games such as Fortnite or League of Legends generate billions of dollars. Players invest money and put their earnings in an infinity pit. Their bank accounts will become depleted when they stop playing games like this.

This is modified by playing-to-earn. Everything collected has value in money. So, players will continue to earn money, even if they're not actively playing the game.

What are the effects of play-to-earning games on the economic landscape?

When we hear "globalization," we immediately connect it to government policies and immigration agreements, trade agreements, and huge corporations. But, the majority of global networking takes place out of boardrooms with virtual spaces accessible from any part of the world. MMO (Massively Multiplayer Online) games have changed how we communicate to build friendships and build communities, by allowing people to interact and share experiences without regard to geographical boundaries in virtual, enjoyable places. A major and interesting aspects of the rapid internationalization of the community is economy that have developed because of it, and the way that players consider and evaluate digital goods and services. Games on the internet, especially MMOs have been at the forefront of new methods of economics that permit global participation. This includes players who want to sell their digital products to earn real-world cash, and large corporations that are developing innovative business strategies.

Virtual Economies' Real-World Applications

Although the practice of buying and selling digital products in exchange for cash isn't new, it is becoming more widespread because online communities have increased in size and morphed into massive enterprises. Venezuela was the subject of international attention as a lot of its residents shifted to farming gold as their primary source of income, recognizing that it could provide more financial security than traditional employment. This practice has increased popular to the point that it comes with it's individual Wikipedia as well as an Encyclopedia Britannica entry.

The majority of businesses in the game have strict Terms of Service (ToS) agreements that restrict Gold Farming and other forms of financial exchanges for in-game items or account transfers. Although these strategies are designed to protect the players but they're more likely to be employed to ensure the control of the economy in game and reduce the risk of being exposed to KYC/AML regulations and increase revenue. These restrictions prohibit a player from gaining value from the assets he or she acquires or earns through games. Because of the restrictions on trade, players cannot sell items they previously purchased and thereby revealing that they don't actually control the products they buy. These strategies have forced certain participants into grey market, where they are exposed to the risk of being a victim of a counterparty and may be shut down in the event of being they are caught.

If there is no valid open and transparent exchange of products is it difficult for gamers to collect the costs that are incurred from prior purchases, let alone earnings from their accounts as well as virtual goods they acquire while gaming. In at the conclusion of the day the closed system could hinder the growth of gaming communities since game companies control their development.

As blockchain technology expands across the globe and new game-based economic models are developing. In the year 2020 the Philippines saw a huge influx of gamers who were not traditional into video games based on cryptocurrency to earn money during COVID-19 lockdowns.

Single moms, grandparents taxi drivers, and even taxi drivers used video games for a way to increase their incomesby developing, building and trading digital commodities which they later sold in public blockchain markets to earn cash. What makes these games different against MMOs Gold Farming games is that they are built on open economies, the removal of restrictions on terms of Service, and innovative technology that makes use of Non-Fungible tokens (NFTs) that run via the Blockchain. These innovative models restore players their power through facilitating control of assets that they purchase and earn.

The System is being played

When early video games moved from traditional boxed games to online services with continuous play and other online services, the game's design changed. Online games established long-term relationships with their clients which required the development of the economic framework. Subscriptions andlater microtransactions made it possible to make incremental purchases. Unfortunately, a number of areas of game design remained not compatible with the new designs. It was a fact that randomized "Loot Boxes" were a source of motivation and reward in early video games but they weren't associated with commercialization through single-purchase packaged games carts.

When they are advertised as microtransactions certain publishers might be able to make money from the game's random components. If taken to its logical end, this could be classified as gambling. In the majority of cases effective "Free to play" games are based on retaining their most loyal players through the possibility of speeding up the progress of their game. However, this could cause anger for certain players, which can result in the players not being motivated to play and putting the burden of earning money only on a small portion of players. The design of a game that favors high rollers could cause irritation and make it difficult for players to stratify their playing base.

So, what exactly do gamers really enjoy? In the end, the virtual world is very similar to the real world. People love collecting limited-edition objects and expressing their status as a social person through the ability to customize their avatar and virtual world. The industry of cosmetics is estimated to generate $40 billion annually and is expected to continue growing. The introduction of blockchain technology to cosmetics that are paid for and virtual goods can lead to new models of economics for the gaming industry . models that could be dominating by non-fungible tokens which allow players to own their purchases, while also sharing profits from resales with developers and providing economic value to the gaming community.

What does this mean for the Investing Professionals?

Although many investors rely on large, publicly traded corporations to guide their market, savvy business leaders will watch and watch how the newer, more agile firms perform before they commit to these innovative ways of marketing. Investors who are cautious tend to take a wait-and-see approach which allows independents to test the waters and assess the validity of their ideas. The strategy is usually to join later, after new models are in place and profitable.

It's a rare opportunity for independent developers, entrepreneurs and investors to join the ground floor. Although creator-based economies aren't new, blockchain technology could enhance existing models of economic development and boost development to new levels. Cryptoeconomics provides gamer communities with the chance to be part of the success of games they enjoy.

The world is watching the current crypto and NFT excitement, and is anticipating what happens in the coming 12 months. Indeed, savvy developers and investors are looking ahead to the next three years as the decisive time for this technology and the associated business models. If the development of games with high-quality open-source blockchain-based economies are likely to be the fastest-growing segment of a market worth $200 billion.

How do they come to be even possible?

Are you aware of instances where you were yelled to by parents playing video games on an electronic device, computer or mobile phone as a child? Parents generally do not approve of video games designed for teenagers, children or even young adults. It is true that it is an entertainment option which helps individuals relax after a long day. But, many people believe that it's a waste of time and possibly cash.

The majority of video games require players to pay to play them. The business model of free-to-play has seen a rise in popularity in recent times. Because games that are free-to-play are accessible for download, you do not have to purchase a subscription to play. However, they often contain optional features or products that you need to buy to enhance your experience or to advance your position within the sport. You're basically investing money in something that won't provide no benefit in the end.

Maybe you're wondering what it could be like if you could flip a switch to make money playing games. Here's some exciting information. It's now possible! Take a look at the play-to earn and NFTs, or non-fungible tokens (NFTs) business models that are the basis for this intriguing idea.

Business Model Based on Play-to Earn

Recently, the play-to-earn model has been introduced in the gaming industry, and has sparked huge interest, particularly among players and those suffering financial difficulties as a result of the problem. The games that are play-to-earn powered use smart contracts, which are blockchain-based application that executes an agreement through code when certain requirements meet. The players are granted ownership of digital assets in the game that increase in value when they play and be traded for real cash in the public blockchain market. Coins, cryptocurrencies, or tokens that are non-fungible can be used to create such asset (NFTs). The players are compensated for their effort, time and skills by using a model of play-to-earn-profit as each item they collect during the game is of real-world value that allows players the opportunity to make money. The model is based on the idea that an economy is open and incorporates it into the creation of an in-game economy that will have a major impact on the economy as well as the gaming industry.

NFTs - Non-Fungible Tokens (NFTs) What are They?

The non-fungible tokens (NFTs) are unalterable, distinct, and authentic tokens made on the blockchain to indicate the ownership for non-fungible resources. Non-fungible items can vary from artwork to game elements. NFT records are hard to alter since they are kept in a public ledger distributed or blockchain. This allows us to validate the authenticity of NFTs, and to manage and transfer their ownership and accessibility easily. But it is crucial to understand the danger of NFTs disappearing because of technological issues as this has already been reported. NFTs are simply codes controlled by blockchain-related parties.

Incorporating NFTs in games, gamers have access to exclusive and simple-to-trade assets that they can gain from when the value of the asset rises or falls on the NFT market. The tokens can be linked to different assets as well as various games, meaning they are able to be used in different games should one of the game servers fails.

Since play-to-earn or non-fee-based business models have become popular within the world of gaming, there is numerous games made using these models, including Decentraland as well as Axie Infinity.

Decentraland:

Decentraland is an decentralized virtual universe that is powered by Ethereum. In the virtual world, you can play and interact in the virtual world by playing games and other activities. You can also buy property that you can use to build your markets, stores and settings. Within Decentraland the three tokens employed: MANA, LAND, and Estate. With the help of Decentraland DAO, a decentralized autonomous entity, the website is managed by the users.

Decentraland was first introduced in January 2020. It was an online environment solely owned by the users and managed via a non-decentralized, autonomous entity (DAO). The three tokens used by Decentraland are used to serve a variety of purposes in this game. LAND represents digital parcels of land in the Decentraland environment. Estate is a symbol of merging pieces of digital land. MANA is the Decentraland's principal currency. It is important to note that both estate and LAND are ERC-721 tokens, also known as NFTs however, MANA is an fungible token (ERC-20).

You play as a persona in Decentraland, and can interact with it by buying art at galleries or playing games at casinos as well as visiting the Decentraland University. The most intriguing thing about Decentraland differs from other game currencies that are available, the currency MANA is a real-world currency that can be exchanged for real world cash. It is important to note that the NFT's LAND and Estate aren't interchangeable, but they can be used to create unique products for the world like wearables in the Decentraland environment, which boosts the value of the game characters. Furthermore, all transactions within decentraland Decentraland setting are recorded in the Ethereum blockchain.

To buy land in Decentraland You must make use of MANA In addition, if you purchase two adjoining plots, these may be combined into an estate. Then, you could earn money in the game by renting your property or by constructing attractions on the land. attractions like casinos as well as art museums are well-known methods for making money within the game. Another method of earning money is to purchase land before it is sold at a profit after. As per reports a parcel of land bought for $500 in the early part of 2019, and is currently being sold at $7800.

The value of land is additionally determined by their attractiveness just like land in real life therefore land next to roads or plazas is more desirable than other plots of land.

In contrast to previous games, Decentraland will not be controlled by a central entity rather, by MANA, Land owners, and Estate holders through the DAO. To vote on any protocol changes it is necessary to have an unwrapped MANA or WMANA. The wrapped MANA can't be spent or transferred, however it will grant the player in-game voting rights. Particularly, every MANA is able to grant you about one vote, while each piece of land grants you to approximately 2000 votes. The most intriguing aspect of LAND can be that is it could be utilized in game, unlike MANA which is a stalemate within the DAO. It is important to remember that, while MANA is able to be obtained through conventional cryptocurrency exchanges, such as Binance as well as Coinbase, LAND can only be bought through the marketplace called

Decentraland. Estate however is only available by combining pieces of land. Decentraland is among the first gaming games of this kind which has opened up an entirely new way to play games where players can earn money without having to rely on an centralized organization, keeping the privacy of the players.

Axie Infinity

Axie Infinity can be described as a fighting and breeding game played on Ethereum that lets players take control of monsters, known as Axie's. The aim of the game is to educate everyone about blockchain technology via an enjoyable gaming experience that is based on the concept of the concept of play-to-earn. The Non-Fungible Tokens (NFTs) will be used during the game to grant players with ownership of digital assets like Axie monsters as well as the game's terrain. These NFTs can be traded via public blockchain exchanges in exchange for real cash. Furthermore, all art-related materials as well as Axie data is accessible to any other party, allowing other users and developers to extend their own Axie universe.

Chapter 3: Defi

What is DEFI?

DEFI is an application for decentralized finance that lets you make fast payments online via a financial network that is decentralized. DEFI removes the need for costly middlemen and central authority, and provides end-to-end encryption to guarantee your security. Your personal information as well as financial transactions will remain completely secure and private and allow you to shop without fear.

In countries with poor populations who don't have access to traditional banking services like the population that is not banked within India or Venezuela can also transfer money internationally at low cost and without the need of costly exchange rates through one of the Development Financial Institutions (DEFI).

Our API platform that is open that connects to a variety of front-end service providers, offers the people to access essential financial services without cost.

Third-party apps, such the ones developed by DEFI can be utilized to improve access to financial services to the under- and unbanked people. DEFI also offers an all-in-one solution that can save time and money for our customers.

What kind of products will Be and available?

Our initial offerings will target the market segments of remittances, peer-to-peer lending as well as currency exchange (FX) and the financing of supply chain. We will also offer merchant solutions to these markets along with other areas. Further opportunities in other areas like personal financial (fintech) platforms are being studied through our group. The DEFI token is integrated in the Ethereum blockchain as an utility token that is based upon Ethereum's blockchain technology, which is similar to the way Bitcoin is used.

What are the most likely to be the most important functions of a token utility?

We believe that by having an DEFI token that you'll have full accessibility to the entire DEFI services and be able use your tokens right from the beginning. Our main goal is to let anyone around the world to gain secure accessibility to banking services. Token holders are entitled to discounts in the cost of our financial and financial services. We're also focused on reducing charges for credit card transactions, and also lowering the rates of interest on loans in order to help people use our services.

Who is likely to be interested by DEFI tokens?

Anyone who would like to utilize our platform will require access to our API. Every user will need to sign up with us, which will be directly connected to the blockchain through an application that is decentralized (dApp) (DApp). In order for users to set up their accounts with DEFI they'll need to be able to have DEFI tokens in their possession . This allows them to avail our value-added services which we offer like discounted rates and interest rates.

What is the value at present in this token? DEFI Token?

In our coin offering, one DEFI token is offered at USD 0.50 or equivalent of ETH and BTC. It is because it offers an attractive value proposition to new users and is in line with our pricing strategy for fees and is in accordance with the current standards in the industry We believe that this cost per token will be the most appropriate alternative. The price per token could increase in the event that greater DEFI tokens are released over time as a result of purchases or participation on our platform, however it is unlikely to fall below USD 0.25 per token.

How can I get involved as a participant in an First Coin Offering (ICO)?

You can purchase DEFI tokens using various exchanges and also using your own bank account If you choose to do this. Specific instructions for creating DEFI tokens through our system will be available in the future. We are currently planning to provide DEFI tokens available for trading across a variety of exchanges in the near future.

If you are having trouble getting your tokens, contact us at [emailprotectedwith details of your address and email, including the type of exchange you made use of, and the name of the firm used to purchase the token. Our team will respond in the quickest way to resolve any issues that you might encounter when purchasing a product or signing up to create the platform.

What's the procedure to utilize my DEFI token?

If you have DEFI tokens stored in your wallet, you'll be able to pay with DEFI tokens on our platform. It is possible to use Ethereum's blockchain to lend or transfer funds to other individuals as well as the transaction will be stored on the blockchain the same time it gets credited to your bank account.

Are There Any Consequences If My Account Isn't In Balance?

If you make use of DEFI tokens to add funds to your account, for example when you make an advance loan or transfer of funds or transferring money, we will charge to your account the DEFI tokens that you used to make the transfer. If you do not have enough DEFI tokens available in your account we'll make use of the money from a previous transaction or transfer to fill up the balance of your DEFI accounts with the balance of tokens.

For each transaction I make I will have a separate wallet for me?

Yes, all the transactions you make will be stored on the Ethereum blockchain which is totally safe. You can store all your transactions and funds on the Ethereum blockchain because it's decentralized, removing the necessity to set up multiple wallets. If you choose to purchase DEFI tokens in the ICO You will receive an email confirmationthat you need to confirm within 24 hours in order to finish the purchase.

After you've verified your identity, then you will be able to access your wallet and can utilize your wallet for transferring DEFI tokens into us in order to help fund your account. In case you've got any queries or concerns regarding the process of obtaining DEFI tokens through an exchange, don't hesitate to contact us.

When DEFI is operational When can I benefit from the savings it brings?

Based on the number of DEFI tokens you hold in your account The cost for conducting business using our service is determined. More tickets that you own in your account, the more number of discounts and services that are value-added that are available to you.

Certain aspects that define the proposition DEFI offers in the world of business, we believe that the following are among them. If you purchase tokens during the initial coin sale (ICO) and you pay interest, your rate will be reduced when you pay because we will cut the costs of transactions.

You will receive an email confirmation of the purchase, which you need to verify within 24 hours in order to finish your purchase. Once you've confirmed your identity, you'll be able to access your wallet , and be able in order to send DEFI tokens into us in order to pay for your account.

DEFI and NFT

An Non-Fungible token (NFT) is an cryptocurrency that was created by the Ethereum blockchain. Each NFT is unique from other. Each token is valued differently and NFT can't be exchanged for another one with the same value.

Take it into consideration in the same way as the baseball trading card or Comic book character. Each character or card is unique and has distinct specific characteristics and features that separate them from others and are an asset to the person who owns it, but completely useless for anyone other. It is the same when it comes to non-financial transactions. Only those with permission to make use of an NFT is able to trade it and no one else can put it into their wallet unless they are authorized to make use of it. It will be an element of their collection until the end of time.

A token called ERC-721 is a digital currency created using the Ethereum blockchain. It can be used to represent physical items to

46

exchange for a cryptocurrency. In many instances the use of these tokens is to represent assets that are already established. For instance, if you own gold bullion. You can put it into your bank account by buying an ERC-721 token which represents the amount of gold bars you own and placing it into your wallet.

It is also possible to make use of your ERC-721 token in order in order to change ownership on an asset between one bank account and another , by moving the asset from one account to the other. After the funds have been added to an account and are not able to be moved or transferred and they cannot be changed in any other manner. It is not possible to alter the appearance or name of your cryptocurrency token ERC-721.

However An NFT is a type of token you create in order to symbolize an investment that doesn't currently exist within the real world. You are in complete control of the details of the token, from its name as well as the design of receipts once it is saved in your digital wallet. With a distinct NFT for each asset that you can never be concerned about transferability issues or compatibility issues with the NFT of a different user.

An NFT is designed to be the development of a web site by using the HTML and CSS code languages. Beautifully designed websites can be developed using your unique idea of a dream house as the foundation. It is possible to create an NFT to build your dream home by using the tools available through the Ethereum Blockchain and lets you use it in the exact as you would the other tokens of ERC-721, or cryptocurrency.

You are able to change names of the NFT However, you can't separate it and create new NFTs using the pieces already present. You are able to create as many different NFTs as you want however, each is only one asset within your portfolio. If you buy an existing NFT the currency remains within your control for the entire duration the life of your Ethereum wallet, unless a different third party wants to buy yours first.

Chapter 4: Step By Step Step Instructions On Flipping Nfts For Profit

Except for the fact that you've been hidden in a cave you've probably heard about NFTs and the massive disruption they're bringing to the world of computers. The normal month-to-month exchange amounts increased from $64M in the first half of this current year , to over $750 million in the second part of the. In the present, the celebration is continuing to be lively, and we're seeing random Twitter customers selling off their craftsmanship for huge amounts of money. Even though that you won't make that much money however, you are able to be a part of the action and earn some money. What if we jump right into the subject.

What are the Flips?

Flipping is a no-cost method to buy things at a low cost and then selling them quickly to gain. It's been around since the beginning of exchanging cards by flipping, games, and other funnies to gain the benefit of others, and today we're witnessing a massive growth in the NFT sector.

Why do we flip NFTs?

It is possible to flip items NFTs have proven to be extremely valuable, swiftly and attracting a variety of financial investors. Apart from keeping Bitcoin as well as Alts or creating and accumulating tokenized work in the shortest time possible and you must get in on the largest volume NFT projects to earn faster profits. While it's not a safe option the flipping of NFTs is generally a quick way to boost your portfolio.

Step-by-step instructions on how for how to Spot Hot NFT Projects

Similar to any other financial market, making gains requires analyzing the measures to determine the most appropriate option. In the majority of cases people tend to choose assets that are undervalued or are hoping to grow in value.

When it comes to NFTs, you'll need to find your area of expertise and perform a thorough exam. Common specialties include creature-themed art, dynamic artwork and collectibles, names of areas and online parcels.

Three crucial measures are the ones that determine the extent to which an NFT enterprise will fare. They include:

The quantity of items: a shortage always drives requests up. NFT projects that have a limited number of items are more likely to yield benefits

Floor Price: Floor value refers to the lowest price you could get for a product. It is important to look for items with minimal floor costs and a small stocks.

Volume: generating gains for any industry is firmly dependent on the liquidity. You must pitch your speculations on stages that have large exchange quantities. Chances are that you'll soon find buyers willing to buy your items.

Where to Look for NFT Projects

1.Special zones on NFT stages

NFT stages are effectively helping clients find potentially lucrative sources. For example those in the "Top Artists" and "Select Drops" areas on AirNFTs are excellent places to check out when you are thinking of buying. The pages on Activity and Rankings on OpenSea also provide some insight regarding possible tasks.

2.Social media

Free alpha is currently all over the world thanks to web-based media. It is likely that artisans and other NFT forces to reckon with a regular announcement of innovative ventures via their social media pages, which include Twitter, Reddit, Telegram, Discord and Instagram. It is sensible idea. Furthermore, NFT stages have web-based media accounts that they use to help their clients' businesses.

Beginning

Flipping NFTs is a simple interaction. You will require an Web3 suitable wallet such as Metamask as well as Trust Wallet. After you have financed your account, you are able to reach different NFT stages using the application program. AirNFTs is the perfect place to begin your flipping endeavor. It is possible to purchase NFTs for extremely low costs for gas and make significant profits through them due to our constantly developing and vibrant local market.

In the event of an offer, it's essential to be aware of when to sell your flipper as flippers. Although the decision is entirely on you, it's important to evaluate the amount and the recognition the job is receiving while at the same considering whether to move in other endeavors.

Be aware that NFTs tend to not be as flexible as their fungible counterparts that is, you could earn a profit only in the event that you can see buyers who are able to buy. In the end, it is important to ensure that you contribute only the risk you could lose.

Top NFT Marketplaces

If you're planning to take part in the NFT excitement, an NFT commercial center is the way to participate in the buying and selling of these resources that are advanced - from music to craft to entire virtual universes. Take into consideration NFT commercial centers to be your Amazon (NASDAQ:AMZN) in the world of advanced technology.

There are a lot of NFT commercial centers operating and many of them are specialized. specialization or focus. What are the most appropriate areas to research before deciding which one to use and which are the most reputable NFT commercial centers that are available? That's what you need to be aware of.

Selecting an NFT commercial center

First, remember that an NFT (non-fungible token) only addresses the responsibility of a resources. Prior to deciding on an NFT commercial centre first, you'll need to determine the type of resource that you're interested to purchase or selling or creating. Anything that is technologically advanced - the written word, recordings computers, computer games, workmanship or other government items such as these can be tokenized using blockchain (like Ethereum (CRYPTO:ETH), the most well-known blockchain platform NFTs are based upon) which means that cutting down your disadvantage is a good place to start.

Another idea is the kind of tokens that are used in commercial premises. Certain tokens support a range of tokens. Others are commercial centers that are closed that use a specific token. When opening an NFT commercial center's record ensure that you fund your blockchain wallet using the correct cryptocurrency or token required to participate in the activities of the site. It will prompt you to connect your wallet with NFT's NFT commercial center once you open a new record. Additionally, you should verify the security measures the commercial center has in its operation, and also if there were any problems in the past.

Ten of the best NFT commercial centers

Here is a selection of the best NFT commercial centers in the moment.

1.OpenSea

OpenSea is the leader when it comes to NFT deals. OpenSea offers a variety of electronic resources that are available as its base and is able to access and browse the many contributions. It also supports artisans and makers. It also has an easy to use process, assuming you want to create an NFT of your own (known in the field of "printing").

The commercial center is backed by over 150 distinct installment tokens, meaning that the name of this stage is appropriate. As a prelude to what is to come in the NFT market, OpenSea is an incredible location to begin.

2.Axie Marketplace

Axie Marketplace is the internet marketplace for the game Axie Infinity. Axies are legendary creatures that can be purchased and then prepared, and later put in competition with Axies of other players to gain rewards. In the Axie Marketplace, players can buy new Axies in a variety of items and terrains as well as NFTs , to be used in the game.

Axie The Infinity tokens (called Axie Shards) are made up of the Ethereum blockchain. In this way, they can be purchased and traded through a variety of NFT commercial centres, the same like on digital currency exchanges such as Coinbase Global (NASDAQ:COIN).

3.Larva Labs/CryptoPunks

Hatchling Labs is most popular for its popular CryptoPunks the NFT initiative. The company was initially sold for nothing in the year 2017 but some CryptoPunks were sold for huge amounts of dollars since then from that point. Hatchling Labs has other computerized crafting projects that are undergoing similar to Autoglyphs and others, as well as many other Ethereum blockchain-based projects for improving applications.

Hatchling Labs' CryptoPunks NFTs are no longer available, however they can be offered for sale and bought from other commercial centers. Also, Larva Labs' different tasks warrant monitoring, including the Meebits which are sold directly from the company's main commercial center.

4.NBA Best Shot Marketplace

NBA Top Shot is the National Basketball Association and Women's National Basketball Association's first introduction to the NFT world. In its commercial center, rare minutes (video clasps and play features) as well as the finest craftsmanship are purchased from the world's top ball associations.

The NBA created it as a commercial shut center (you can buy and sell through Top Shot) utilizing the Flow blockchain created with Dapper Labs. It's easy to join and buy through Top Shot's Top Shot commercial center site. The minutes are available from as little as a few dollars.

5.Rarible

Rarible is a large commercial center with various NFTs like OpenSea. There is a wide variety of work and recordings, collectibles and music are available for purchase as well as sold in the theater. In contrast to OpenSea the stage requires you to make use of Rarible, the center's token called Rarible (CRYPTO:RARI) to buy and sell your items at this commercial centre. Rarible is built in Ethereum. Ethereum blockchain (despite the fact that works of art may be managed by OpenSea as well using Rarible tokens).

The company has collaborated with some exceptional organizations. Yum! Brands' (NYSE:YUM) Taco Bell has documented their work on Rarible and cloud-based programming giant Adobe (NASDAQ:ADBE) at recent collaborated with Rarible to help with obtaining NFT specialists and makers working.

6.SuperRare

Similar to Rarible, SuperRare is additionally developing a commercial center for makers who are advanced. SuperRare offers workmanship as well as recordings as well as 3D images. However, the authorities are able to purchase craftsmanship using Ethereum.

SuperRare has recently announced its own logo with the same name, based upon the Ethereum blockchain. SuperRare NFTs are used to discover and organize new capabilities to the commercial center. Similar to Rarible, SuperRare NFTs can also be bought and traded through OpenSea.

7.Foundation

Foundation.app was designed to provide a straightforward, technical method of offering computerized work. The deals are done using Ethereum. The commercial center's dispersal in mid 2021, it's sold over $100 million worth of NFTs.

Specialists are invited to the stage through the Foundation individuals group, and buyers need only a crypto wallet that's backed by Ethereum to start making purchases. If you're looking for a quick and easy way to start creating your own NFTs, Foundation may not be the best place to begin, but the commercial center is home to an abundance of artwork that you can examine within a simple organisation.

8.Nifty Gateway

Clever Gateway has collaborated with the the most well-known and renowned modern craftsmen, such as Beeple or artist Grimes. It's a stage for curation of craftsmanship powered by the cryptocurrency trade Gemini (constrained through those of the Winklevoss twins).

The NFTs which are also called Nifties are built on Ethereum.

In addition to being an organized stage Nifty Gateway additionally has any NFTs purchased - meaning that NFTs aren't deposited in your personal wallet but actually stored via Nifty Gateway and Gemini. Although this may not be the best option for NFT collectors who require greater flexibility with their particular speculations Nifty purchases and deals are also able to be purchased with government-issued money (e.g., U.S. dollars) without the need to make the purchase first using a digital currency.

9.Mintable

Mintable, backed by billionaire Mark Cuban, plans to become an open commercial centre similar to OpenSea. If you're interested in buying as well as trading NFTs on Mintable it is necessary to have Ethereum. Mintable also allows the stamping of NFTs by artists of all sorts (from photographers and performers) who wish to market your work to be a high-end resource.

61

A longing NFT maker or authority should purchase Ethereum through a cryptocurrency trade first. At the point of purchase, connect their account with Mintable for use with buying and selling from Mintable's commercial centre.

10.Theta Drop

Theta is a stage that uses blockchain technology and designed to allow decentralized use of TV and video online. Its NFT commercial centers Theta Drop made its introduction in 2021, along with The World Poker Tour's computer-generated collectibles. The World Poker Tour was the first to adopt ThetaTV and utilizes the stage to stream video.

Theta utilizes its own innovation in blockchain. In order to participate in Theta Drop's Theta Drop NFT commercial center it is necessary to purchase Theta Token (CRYPTO:THETA). Different crypto exchanges, for instance, Binance supports Theta and Theta Tokens, as well as the NFTs and tokens bought using them are able to be put into a crypto wallet similar to the one used by Theta's own crypto wallet app.

The process of putting funds into NFTs

NFT commercial facilities are the best option to start putting money into collectibles, advanced materials as well as work, but there are many options available. Be sure to select one that is compatible with your buying and capacity requirements based on the type of NFT you're looking for and the crypto you're interested on using to exchange.

Also, be aware that this is an entirely different field and is largely theorized. Certain NFTs could rise in price, but there is no guarantee. The value of modern workmanship and collectibles is the same as the actual value of collectibles and workmanship The value of a piece is deductive and is influenced by various variables such as distinctiveness and the status of the craftsman that made the item. Buy a piece of art and assuming that you have your general business plan as well as your total assets, and a speculation time line as your primary concern.

Chapter 5: Understanding Nft

The Value unlocking the Powers of NFT

What is the reason why I am so convinced about NFTs?

The most important technological advances over the past 20 years were derived from the ability to unlock the frozen assets that were frozen, and NFTs are the perfect illustration of this. For investors and entrepreneurs this is an important mental model. Some examples:

Airbnb

Airbnb unlocked underused residential real estate. The concept of this was that if you own an apartment or a home that has a sofa, every night you're not in use from 10 pm to 6 am is comparable to taking a fifty-dollar note and putting the fire to it. Extra room? Perhaps you'll get a Benjamin.

Uber

Uber unlocked and un-used time. Are you in search of an hour or two in between working hours? Uber makes use of mobile devices that are location aware to allow you to work for a short period as an Uber driver or courier.

Facebook

Facebook utilized two different assets that were frozen. The first was an account on the Facebook graph. It's interesting to observe that users on social networks are mostly seeking to connect with others who have something in common.

The first asset that was to be stored was human relationships that were not yet digitalized. The second was data on behavior. Facebook keeps track of your activities both on and off the platform, and uses the data to generate automated content.

When you publish your article, or include a hashtag an image, the results of these interactions generate new content that you can send to your acquaintances. FB is more proficient in repurposing information than other platforms, which is why they're the best platform.

Google

In fact, Google didn't come up with backlinks at all They simply sifted through the data that was already available and used it to produce a 10 fold increase in search results. Understanding how to recognize frozen assets that are able to be removed from the freezer is the best way to earn money from technology.

What are the advantages that NFTs can unlock?

The most obvious answer is an online talent, that is why we need to begin with this.

Three of the key innovations the basis of NFTs are.

1.) Artists can create limited editions of digital products.

2.) They make it simple to authenticate

3.) Artists earn money through the sale of their work to customers who are secondary.

In order to become an artist you've got to convince a gallery or gatekeeper to go for the boundaries of. With NFTs, artists may instead sell their work for an affordable cost or even for no cost and earn money through the sale of their products to secondary markets once their work is admired.

When artists receive compensation by the impact of their work on the world and their impact on the world, they can be able to create a new generation people who are able to earn an income and impact our society. NFTs provide control and power over artists.

A lot of people have worked for years, or even decades to acquire the capacity and skills of creating artwork that can help people to see the world in a different way. NFTs allow them to work full-time and earn money as artists. Innovative technology lets you unlock the value of an asset that was frozen.

I'm guessing that there are more frozen assets available currently such as new goods and services that are already in existence but could be viable economically due to clear, precise and solid price determination. We'll be able to provide more details regarding this in the near future.

What's happening in the present moment? Companies that are built around frozen assets generally have specificities and we can make use of these particularities to figure out the place we are working on applying technology.

The first thing to note is that the majority of people who have assets frozen aren't convinced that they have stored their assets. The process of convincing them to do so is vital to achieving the success of your business. It took many years to convince Airbnb to convince people that rooms not being used could be sold.

In contrast to SaaS companies that grow by X% each month, companies that are based that have frozen assets may go from being in a state with not having a need for months, or even years, to experiencing rapid growth in just a couple of minutes.

Many people believe these dollar-sized bills found on the streets are real, but when some people learn that they are not, everybody quickly realizes the error as they fight tooth and nails for the coins.

It's exactly what we're seeing now. Everyone from actors to celebrities recognizes that there's plenty of money to be made by NFTs. They're searching for the most efficient method to make it happen.

The producers of these well-known shows have all spoken about their collaboration in conjunction with each other And, as of now they're all aware of the idea of the launch of NFT initiatives NFT idea is an excellent idea. They're trying to learn the technical aspects of how to initiate projects in order that they don't harm their image.

From an investment standpoint From an investment perspective, a bet on a business must represent an investment into the assets of the company rather than an individual approach. Should Uber black cars weren't profitable, they could have chose to offer taxis. If they had not been able to fail they could have launched Uber Eats. Or Instacart.

The whole industry is based on exactly freezing of assets (time and location). It

69

utilizes similar technology that makes it affordable to switch from one application to another until you've reached oil. (Another classic tale of frozen assets is this time, from 1859.)

Like Uber, NFT technology can be utilized in a range of ways. It is possible to do it quickly and cost-effectively. There will be lots of tests, and more will be realized. The most memorable example of this week is from the twitter account of @punk6529:

I'm not sure what's going to be the most well-known and commercial artist who is successful in this NFT period. I'm not certain that it will be art that is the most popular application. But I am sure that there are plenty of talented individuals that will soon create digital content that earns money.

For every Zaha Hadid, there are 100 other people working on the Gen art industry are equally talented , yet they cannot earn money by convincing others to transform their art into the building. They can also have extremely lucrative careers. That's how.

The Xx SerSBonus: What frozen assets can be unlocked using the most recent technology or technology that is expected to release in next years?

What do you want to be able to unlock and which ones are the most profitable?

Chapter 6: Trading And Creating Nfts

It is clear that the NFT market is full of opportunities for investors and content creators. In this article, you will be introduced to the process of how you can develop your own NFT and how you can begin trading and buying NFTs for sale.

6.1 Create a MetaMask Wallet

When creating NFTs You will need be able to contribute fees to the blockchain's network that you're using. The most common blockchain on which NFTs are made is Ethereum and gas charges are required in order to tokenize your artwork. To begin, you'll first create an MetaMask wallet. MetaMask wallets are available by visiting metamask.io free of charge. This is where you'll be able to transfer Ether to pay for gas. The NFTs you buy will be tied to the ID in your account. When you create your wallet, you'll receive the seed phrase. The seed phrase is very importantas it could be used in the case that you require to retrieve your wallet. For the best security, write your seed word on a piece of paper and store it in a safe place. Your private key to your wallet must be secure, since they are required to signify transactions.

6.2 Tokenizing your Art

After you have created your MetaMask wallet You are now in a position to issue your artwork in the form of an NFT. The procedure that will be explained will be based on OpenSea. OpenSea platform. To set up an NFT through OpenSea visit opensea.io and click on the Create button in the main menu. Then, you will be connected to your MetaMask wallet to OpenSea. After that, you will be able to make a name for the NFT collection. If you are creating the first collection you create using your account at OpenSea then you'll need to pay a gas cost with Ethers. You can send Ethereum directly to your MetaMask wallet, if you already have one, or purchase Ethereum via cryptocurrency exchanges like Coinbase as well as Gemini.

Inside the library, you'll be able add new items. If you click on"Add New Item" Add New Item button, you'll have the option of uploading the file in digital format that you would like to tokenize. When you do this you'll be able define the particular properties for every file, as well as the statistics of the brand new NFT. The final step in tokenizing your work would be to decide the quantity of copies you would like from your NFT and the price it retails at. Congratulations! You just made your first NFT.

6.3 Selling your NFT sale

If you're planning for a way to market your NFT You can make it happen on OpenSea. OpenSea platform. You'll need to activate the selling feature of your account with OpenSea. Once you've given the platform the authority for selling your NFTs the NFTs will be available to anyone to purchase and find.

6.4 NFT Creation on Rarible

Alongside OpenSea You can also make use of Rarible to create your own NFTs too. Both platforms excel in aiding users in tokenizing their artwork without having to have any technical expertise to conduct transactions on the blockchain. The

Rarible platform is better suited for artists looking to create a handful of NFTs to market them at premium prices due to the lower cost of production. OpenSea is a better choice for those trying to make a collection of less expensive NFTs since it will make it cheaper to build an entire collection of NFTs using its platform.

6.4.1 Connecting your wallet

If you'd like to use tokenization for your content through Rarible instead, visit Rarible.com and link your wallet to the site. On Rarible you are able to connect various types of wallets, including MyEtherWallet or Fortmatic. You may also opt for connecting to your Coinbase Wallet to it, which makes it easier for buying Ethereum and paying fuel costs.

6.4.2 Collectibles Creating

Now you can begin to create an NFT by pressing"Create. Then, you will be asked to select between making Single or Multiple editions of your work. Single editions mean the creation of only one edition (NFT) for your artwork will be made that adds distinctiveness and exclusivity. However when you're looking to market your artwork repeatedly, you may choose the multiple option. Then, you will be able to upload documents in various formats including png, mp4 as well as gif, jpeg, and png. Then, you can modify the specifications, such as royalty amounts and prices for sale.

When you've found the specifications you want and then you are able to begin the process to make your NFT. When you click the Create button and your file will begin to upload. After the files are completely uploaded, you will be able begin making your own NFT. The process of minting your NFT will require gas charges. You have the option of altering the cost of gas, which is in direct proportion to the transaction time. A higher gas price will enable transactions to be processed fast, while lower charges will result in longer processing times. This is why it is suggested to choose the slower option so that you'll be in a position to save more on the cost of gas. You can also enter your own gas costs however, it is not recommended to select the lowest price because it could mean the transaction won't be processed in any way. The NFT will then be credited to your account after the transaction has been completed. The NFT will be immediately offered for auction.

6.5 Buy NFTs

The majority of transactions by NFT marketplaces make use of Ethereum as the main method for value transfer. The first step for purchasing NFTs is to buy Ethereum that you'll be using to conduct transactions through these marketplaces. The Ethereum that you have will need to be transferred to a wallet which can be linked to the market where you would like for an order to acquire an NFT.

6.5.1 Marketplaces NFT

There are many NFT marketplaces that are available with various NFTs that are available for purchase. Explore these marketplaces to discover the NFT you'd like to purchase, prior to connecting your account to the marketplace. The most well-known NFT marketplaces are

OpenSea, SuperRare, NBA Top Shot, Nifty Gateway and Sorare. Certain marketplaces are specifically targeted at a particular niche and thus may have better high-quality NFTs in that particular area that are available for auction. For instance, NBA Top Shot specializes in licensed NBA collectibles, and you'll be more likely to being able to find NBA related NFT that you are searching for on the platform.

6.5.2 Making an purchase

After you've decided on the platform you'd like to place the purchase, connect your account with the site and ensure you have enough money in the account to make the purchase. In the majority of cases, transactions are made on bidding systems, in which you'll need to make a bid on the NFT you'd like to purchase.

Chapter 7: What Is Nft?

I'll begin by describing this scenario: if I loan you $100 in cash and then I return two $50 notes. It's great to accept it because it has the same value to the $100 loaned you, even though it's from different banks. I'm able to call this is a fungible. Simply put, everything you swap or exchange will have the identical value. In the example I provided above, it can be interchangeable with bitcoin, gold, Ethereum or Casino. However it is a non-fungible asset which cannot be replaced or substituted because it has a distinct value that makes it different from other assets within the same asset class. One example is an art work as well as a theater ticket, trademark skin for a video game.

Certain of these assets are real and tangible, while others are intangible and digital. Therefore, NFTs are not fungible. tokens are a type of digital certificate stored by a secure blockchain, a distributed database. So NFTs are digital assets that are publicly verified intellectual property verified on blockchain. One of the most popular places to investigate a wide range of NFTs can be found at opensea.io

This photo of a cat was auctioned for 18 000. You can't imagine!

You may be wondering, what the reason is? It's only an image formatted in Jpeg that is able to be copied, emailed or uploaded online and duplicated however many times we'd like. But, no, this is not a replicable image since this can only be used as an NFT. The image is able to be reproduced but it doesn't hold the same significance as the original digital art since it is an NFT token that is used to preserve authenticity and value.

If you have purchased a Picasso and you've seen it, you're buying an art canvas that has painting on it. The thing that makes this painting unique is the fact that the person who painted it the canvas was Picasso. It is fact that there is only one canvas that has paint on it in this particular manner. This is the reason it is very rare, and it can only be possess by one individual.

In the past one year NFTs (also known as cryptocurrency art) has drastically changed the art scene and has been celebrated with a lot of money. The technology has revolutionized the art scene. It may sound like hyperbole however, in this particular case there's something to be said about it. If you're creating digital art in any form it is likely that you be aware of what crypto art is and the opportunities it could offer your work. This is why I'm going to do my best to understand the concept and make it clearer.

Let's do this! NFT (non-fungible token).

The reason the token can't be duplicated is due to the fact that it's within the system of blockchain. Blockchains are a digital recording of transaction. It's an informational list in its simplest form. I am given money by someone else. as well as a note of the transaction on a document. I use the money for something other. Recordings are made from the listing.

Blocks are the records which are linked together to create a huge old list. Each record has to be checked by multiple computers. This means that the system that is able to join in and invalidate the chain or even make it up. This is how bitcoin and cryptocurrency function. It is possible to create the digital proof of ownership of money by using the blockchain. It is possible to create this for all kinds of other objects, too which is precisely the kind of thing people are doing using art.

You can determine the owner of each of these pieces. The owner is able to sell it, or lease the rights to a museum for the display of it, or even decide the conditions in the conditions under which the piece is displayed.

What are the differences between NFTs and cryptocurrency?

The reason cryptocurrency and blockchain have gained popularity is due to their uncentralized nature. It is not necessary to have any authority's approval to utilize cryptocurrency or Ethereum. There isn't a central authority with the authority to take away your NFT however, you will still require permission from a third party to use it , or at the very least, access the funds. If, for instance, you purchase an NFT that is a virtual sword in an online game, it is likely that you won't be allowed to use it outside of the game , or at the very least, without permission from the game's publisher. The interesting thing about NFTs is that they're like cryptocurrencies, and their value is determined by the scarcity of them, and therefore could appreciate even though there could just have one bitcoin. There could be a lot of words in a game, therefore, you can sell your sword to exchange for Ethereum or some other token on an exchange , or maybe you could use it to make a second purchase from the same website.

How can you convert your digital token into token

What can you do with this work of digital artwork you have designed and transform it into something that has the token others would want to purchase? Certain marketplaces and websites allow you to upload your artwork and then upload it to the blockchain, and then sell it on their website like Opensea. Opensea is likely to be the most user-friendly website for newbies.

They're incredibly easy to use and jump into. When browsing the artwork on this website is a great way to discover a variety of mostly pop art and memes which are just running through photoshop filters large amounts of bitcoin fan art, basic 3D models that are being sold as collectibles However, I am not able to judge what constitutes art. One thing is for certain is that , the less the bar for anyone to gain access there are more users will be jumping into the site with whatever it is they like hoping to earn quick cash.

It's where the story becomes exciting. There are websites that are more curator-driven sites such as superrare and Niftygateway. These are more traditional galleries, or dealers that curate artworks and artists that they exhibit and sell. It is the place where well-known digital artists are earning money. The auction house, known for its high-end art as well as collaborating with Beeple artist Beeple and is currently preparing to sell his work to an art market that is more traditional. This comes following Beeple has made 3.5 million in December, with an art sale was hosted on Niftygateway. It's not only Beeple. Numerous online artists are making a profit and making a ton of money by selling their work on this platform in the past few months.

How do I buy NFTs.

Let's say you're looking to start the process of building your NFT collection. You'll need an electronic wallet that permits you to keep NFTs. In addition, you might be required to buy cryptocurrency in order to purchase NFTs. It is recommended to purchase Ether since it is among the most popular cryptocurrency that can be used to buy NFTs.

1. Create the Ethereum purchase.

Since most NFTs are Ethereum-based tokens the majority of collectibles markets accept Eth tokens for payment. You can purchase Ethereum via the cryptocurrency exchange and add it in your MetaMask wallet in the event that you already have an account with a cryptocurrency exchange.

Coinbase along with eToro are excellent options for beginners in the event that you don't have a cryptocurrency exchange account.

2. Utilize OpenSea or an equivalent NFT Marketplace in order to join to your MetaMask.

NFTs can be purchased and sold on a range of sites. It is possible to purchase various types of art or collectibles based on the marketplace you select. These sites include secondary markets, which offer a broad variety of NFTs, but each one operates in a different way.

The MetaMask wallet can be described as an Ethereum wallet that is accessible via the Chrome extension or mobile application. A Ethereum account is needed to sign in to OpenSea (and the other NFT websites). Download MetaMask and create a wallet and send the ETH that you bought through Coinbase over. Go through the no-cost Crypto & DeFi 101 tutorial for a thorough video tutorial for those who are making this their first experience with cryptocurrency wallets.

* OpenSea is an Ethereum-based exchange for tokens that are not fungible. Customers can swap tokens that are not fungible for crypto on the network. It offers everything from video games to digital art. A cryptocurrency wallet on the web such as MetaMask is required to use the platform. Your Ethereum wallet's address is used as an login and password to various services, such as OpenSea. It is now time to begin investigating the market and making bids once you have connected your wallet.

Here are some more of the most famous NFT exchanges:

* Super Rare is an NFT-specific social platform. Every item sold that is offered on the platform is unique and customers can purchase and sell these exclusive items through the website of the

company. You'll need to make a deposit on your account using Eth tokens in order to buy items since the site is based on the Ethereum network.

* The largest cryptocurrency exchange Gemini is the owner of Nifty Gateway Nifty Gateway, which operates as the NFT marketplace. Famous artists such as Steve Aoki, Grimes, 3LAU, and many others work with the platform to sell works on the main marketplace. Collectors can resell their art through the secondary marketplace of the company. It is possible to utilize Ethereum to pay for the Nifty accounts, and make use of the site to connect your credit card.

* NBA Top Shot is a licensed NBA market for collectibles. These basketball cards have more of an interactive feel than normal trade cards, and also offer unique twists of basketball-themed cards. Highlights of games played by the players who are highlighted such as the NBA Top Shot, for instance, are displayed within the packs. The LeBron James Dunk-themed card that showed footage of James playing

against Houston Rockets Houston Rockets and sold for more than $200,000. It was the highest-priced card that was sold by NBA Top Shot.

3. Purchase the NFT

After your account is cleared, purchasing an NFT is an easy process. You'll need to make a place a bid for the NFT you want to purchase because most markets function as auctions. For NFTs with multiple printing, some markets operate as exchanges, employing the highest bid as well as the lowest demand.

The possibility of resales value for an NFT bought directly from the marketplace is a benefit. Certain high-demand NFTs can fetch up to five to 10 times their initial price within a short time after their launch. The downside of purchasing NFTs on the market is that it's difficult to anticipate the demand. You can compare your purchase to previous purchases made in secondary market.

How do you view your NFTs

When you visit your account page on the web, you will find your newly purchased

NFT on the desktop of OpenSea's website or within the MetaMask smartphone wallet. If you plan to purchase additional NFTs it is possible to alter your profile's name and image to enable people to find and view your portfolio.

If you decide to purchase from a specific collection, we recommend following the creator's social media to keep informed of the plans for the future of the project as well as any updates in the future. The majority of NFT collections come with an official Twitter account with links to official sites as well as the Discord server on which token holders can talk and converse with each other in private chats.

Chapter 8: Reasons For Sorge

There's more to it than just roses and wine. There are plenty of reasons to be cautious even if informed and can see the benefits. Every risk has its own drawbacks such as NFTs and cryptocurrency, and they aren't an exception to this. There's a lot over-hyped and exaggerated claims regarding the risks of cryptocurrency markets. The majority of these are exaggerated, but even those which are exaggerated do have advantages. It is essential to tackle these since problems can't be resolved until they are recognized.

and Pollution and Pollution

Recently, there's been a significant amount of interest paid to the amount of energy needed for maintaining blockchains. Blockchain is an extremely clever and useful technology, however it's energy-inefficient. Although two banks can transfer just a little bit of information to each other however, the blockchain needs many powerful computers with a lot of power to compete one another.

If you've seen headlines in the news in recent times, this topic isn't controversial. News generates revenue by generating attention with appealing headlines and nuanced debates don't attract the same volume of traffic as doom and gloom tales. However, the facts about pollution do not have any consensus. There is a lively debate about this issue, with both sides having strong arguments that have to be examined.

The majority of the information comes from one source: an academic study published that appeared in Nature Climate Change. The article of 2018 raised concerns about the possibility that Bitcoin alone could raise world's temperature 2 degrees Celsius in the next 30-60 years, which is enough to start increasing the temperature of the ocean to dangerous levels (Dittmar and Praktiknjo, 2019,).

Since these authors have a background in climate science, is not experts in computer science, the authors make assumptions that aren't dependable. For instance, they suppose that the exponential growth of crypto will last for a long time. This isn't an assurance. There aren't many things that grow exponentially for the rest of time and unabated. The majority of growth shows periods of peak and valleys, as well as times of flattening.

It also commits a serious error when it states it is true that the Bitcoin network is able to process 1 billion transactions that is a lot more than the amount Bitcoin is able to do. It also presumes that each transaction is equivalent to one block. As we have discussed previously, one block can contain numerous transactions, more than 3,000 transactions can be included in a block in Bitcoin.

The article states that one Bitcoin transaction will require more power than 750,000 swipes on credit cards. It's true, however electronic banking transactions encompass much more than signals that are sent out by swipes at retail stores. Credit card and bank companies have infrastructure. These companies have office spaces, company vehicles, ATMs and customer service systems and many more which also consume energy, however aren't considered in the calculations.

The numbers also assume Bitcoin energy is derived solely via fossil fuels. A lot of crypto mining companies make use of coal as the primary energy source for a large amount of work they perform. This is definitely something that's troubling and should be phased out however it's not a matter that is specific to computing. It's important to note that the numbers insist that ALL energy is used that way, but this isn't the case.

Miners are encouraged to cut the expense of mining through cutting down on energy consumption. Once a certain level is reached the energy cost is too high, the mining profits would be at an unsustainable level, and mining will cease. The efficiency of energy used by mining equipment is improving but the paper does not discuss this.

The precise numbers of the energy used isn't yet known and estimates vary from

40-440 Terawatts-hour each year. According to Cambridge their most reliable estimate is around 130TWh (CBECI 2021) This is exactly the same amount as the energy used to mine gold each year.

There are some innovative ideas you can make cryptocurrency more sustainable. Computer farms used by miners generate an enormous amount of heat from the energy they consume . These miners are working on ways to make use of this heart as a form of energy by itself.

Renewable energy has lots of potential, however in the moment, they're stuck at technology limitations that hinder them from becoming the norm. Wind and solar energy could generate huge amounts of energy when there is sunshine and winds are blowing, far more than what's needed to power the grid at the same time. If the sun doesn't shine or the winds aren't blowing it produces no energy. We do not have the technology to store huge quantities of energy. The amount of battery storage needed isn't practical yet. In periods of high demand, the extra energy could be used specifically towards mining. The cryptocurrency generated could be reinvested in the energy company in order to increase renewable energy.

Don't believe that crypto doesn't have any impact on the natural environment. It's not true in any way. It is true that there are valid concerns regarding this subject however it's not to be the climate doomsday scenario media headlines suggest it is.

Bubbles

The regulation of crypto isn't as strict as banks are. We are in the final stage of the Wild West crypto economy. The market is full of inherent volatility and the potential to be controlled by both private and government officials using the money to put the weight of their bodies around.

Tweets from people such as Elon Musk can spike or make the crypto market go down with huge margins (Kau 2021). This could be unintentional or even deliberate. One method of manipulating the market to gain profit is to allow an "whale," a well-financed entity or person that is able to buy lots of cryptocurrency. They will require lots of funds to accomplish this However, if crypto is getting bought rapidly and in large amounts then the price will go up. This creates a shortage, and boosts the confidence of people in the worth of the investment, which makes more people are eager to get involved and increase the value. The portfolio of the whale will rise up. When they spot that it is descending it is possible for the whale to dump their portfolio for lots of money, which will lower the value. The market is able to see the price going down and then panic to sell. When it is at its lowest the whale is able to purchase it at a bargain. The process could be repeated for a long time. It's naive to think that governments don't participate.

Bubbles are a normal part of every market however, crypto is a particular exception. It is a relatively new phenomenon, and it is unregulated and is in its early stages. The traditional banking system has invested enormous amounts of money into studying how to assess risks, protect it, and how to maximize profits and has created a vast collection of financial instruments that maximise profits and ensure that the market is secure enough for people to are confident to work within it, with the least risk. Crypto isn't as advanced. It's more like someone who is young, stepping into the front door, claiming that the older people do not know what they're talking about and attempting to do everything in one go. The crypto-culture is correct in a lot of ways and is also likely to be wrong on a number of things. Certain amounts of time must pass and a certain amount of education is required before the crypto world works itself out.

Legal Grey Area

When there is a severe economic turmoil the people are usually eager to come up with alternatives to the system in turmoil. The Great Depression and the stock market crashes during the Great Depression and stock market crash in America throughout the 30s there was a concern that the policies and spending of the federal government could cause hyperinflation like the type that was seen in Germany. To safeguard themselves from the bad monetary policy of the government and the possibility of a monetary crisis, those who had the ability to do this tried to transform their cash into commodities, specifically gold. Even if cash decreases in this way, the prices of other assets such as gold and land will rises to the equivalent amount thereby protecting the individual from being ripped off of their savings completely to extinction by central banks.

The worth of any currency is contingent on trust and confidence in the currency. When people start to eliminate cash, the worth of the cash in that country decreases. Cash is just like other asset. It is characterized by a supply and demand curve, just like everything else. If people lose confidence in the viability and solvency of a business, the value of its stock plummets. If people lose faith in the future solvency and sustainability of a nation then the worth of the money it holds vanishes.

The United States government was not ignorant of this reality. This is why they sought to stay ahead of the game and decided they had the authority and duty to take gold. According to their thinking, there was no way to get rid of this United States dollar, the value of the currency wouldn't be affected as much. They also introduced a number of rules for financial transactions, some rational but some are crazed in order to safeguard from the United States dollar.

Don't make any mistake. In the event that you think that the United States dollar seems threatened by cryptocurrency, the government are likely to intervene and close it down. This is true for NFTs too. The problem in regulating the digital asset is regulators aren't knowledgeable about computers. The average age of senators of the United States is 64 years old (Cillizza 2021). Most of them have a background in the military or in law. There are hardly any people with a background in the field of technology, excluding perhaps that 2020 candidate for president Andrew Yang, who is not a elected official as of the time of writing.

Other countries, with no prior warning or an awareness of what's going on and have been able to crack the digital currency. In a recent case, India has outlawed cryptocurrencies entirely. This is a reaction to a technology they are worried about the negative consequences and implications of and they consider banning these currencies as a way of getting an early start before it is beyond their control. China has also begun to create their own currency, and outlaw rival currencies, and also to invest in existing cryptocurrency that is already well-known and tested and available in the present. This indicates that China has a clear understanding of the significance of what cryptocurrency is and would like to have in the way of securing the phenomenon and regulate it.

There is no reason to believe the United States governments or any governments across the West should not begin looking into and regulating these issues. Due to the general inadequacy of the government and the people who elect them, we can be sure that any regulation that comes our way, it will be led through established entities with huge pockets that are worried about a new start-up that intends to force the company out of existence due to the process of obsolescence. This is something all investors should seriously think about prior to making a significant investment with NFTs and crypto. There's plenty of risk within these markets due to the fact that this is a relatively new technology that is working on and refining, but there's also another source of instability due to the unpredictable responses from the government. The government typically operates in two different ways: "Do nothing" and "overreact." If senators aren't in an emotional state at the last minute then they are more likely to not act. If they do take action and react, expect an overreaction.

Copyright and illegal Content

Making an NFT doesn't guarantee you a copyright on the artwork. Also, tokenizing the Disney classic Snow White and the Seven Dwarves into a video NFT does not suggest you are entitled to use it, neither. There's nothing to stop individuals from tokenizing content that they are not entitled to or distributing it.

NFT trading websites employ software to look for copyrighted materials and take it down in the event that it's disclosed. All well and good but there's one crucial aspect. Blockchains are forever. When someone uploads data to it, the blockchain cannot be changed. The uploaded content can't be erased. Copyright enforcement is extremely complicated.

It's unclear which courts will rule on copyrights for copying NFTs and whether purchasing an NFT is a sign of ownership over intellectual property. There's currently plenty of speculation that patent trolls have been buying NFTs in the hope of winning this battle in court. The term "patent troll" is someone who earns money by suing corporations with a lot of frivolous claims to patent ownership. IBM is currently working to make patents more recognizable, but the exact meaning of this isn't entirely clear (Mollen 2021).

Assets Versus Currency

As we have discussed previously that crypto isn't an official form of currency legally speaking, despite the fact that it can be traded easily as digital cash.

As cryptos of all kinds and even NFTs are considered assets, they are tax-exempt from capital gains tax. Capital gains taxes require an accounting of the assets which have grown in value, and an amount of tax on that basis regardless of any taxes on the transaction of an NFT. In fact, investing money into NFTs requires you to maintain your paperwork to avoid getting any scrutiny from tax collection agencies, especially in the event that you are able to make it big.

Many products are taxed specifically pertaining to them, and lots of economic and political considerations are considered when drafting the laws. There's no reason why the tax rate shouldn't be altered specifically to focus on this market.

Covenant Contracts

This is a legal question that hasn't received much attention at this point, but is expected to be resolved sooner rather than later. A hundred years prior to that, there was a notion in the law of contracts called exclusionary clauses. They were declared not constitutional in the United States Supreme Court. The way in which these agreements worked was the fact that when contracts were made to sell a home the contract would contain an obligation in which the buyer wouldn't be permitted to sell the property to a person of color and were also obliged to include the identical clause when they sold the house in the future.

The result was that this agreement resulted in a particular home as well as a land parcel forever and irrevocably out of the ownership of any black individual for the rest of their lives. Two persons could enclose a piece of land for a period of the time. Because of obvious reasons, this was deemed to be illegal. In addition to being racist What is the reason that anyone should be able to control the product or land for many years after they have passed away?

The smart contracts mediated by Ethereum blockchain could run into a similar issue before the court. Since the contract is locked in the future, theoretically should Ethereum was able to last for 1000 years, the current rules are going to force people to live in accordance with them for a long time after any party involved are alive.

These sorts of questions are hard for computer scientists and lawyers to comprehend. It is difficult to explain this the presence of a judge to those who don't understand the basics of computers is a problem which will only get harder as we become connected to machines that are complex enough for the average person to comprehend. Juries are experts at the field

of law. They don't know a single thing about computers.
Scams

Not all services and cryptos are created equally.

There are a few cryptocurrency and blockchains that have proven and tested, and dependable and have gained an investor's trust. You've heard of some of them. You might not be aware that there are many more.

Inventing a new cryptocurrency is as simple as copying what others have already completed and it is something that people do every day. Even professional boxer Manny Pacquiao made his own cryptocurrency. Digital currencies are developing quicker than they can be traced. A few of them are minor uncommon, and not widely known, but legitimate. There are some that are absolute scams that claim that you will be rich in Bitcoin in only a short time however, they you'll just be taken by the scammer and then disappear.

To distinguish between the two You must look out for what is or isn't recognized. If you're interested then you should take a look at the whitepaper and take a look. If a person or firm launches a crypto, it is nearly always publish whitepapers. The documents provide information about the cryptocurrency and the goals it has. It also contains technical details about the way it operates, and also addressing issues with other crypto assets this one is trying to resolve. They also contain commercial and financial information that can help investors find it. They are generally written made in plain English, which means it doesn't require you to be an knowledgeable to comprehend them.

The majority of cryptocurrency, such as Ethereum or Bitcoin produce more coins on their own however, some coins are created completely by the person who created the cryptocurrency. They could simply force the cryptocurrency into existence at the press of a button. They then have to wait for it to rise to whatever level they desire, and then sell their assets and dump the market and switch to a different project before repeating the same thing. This has been played out many times. Every person who didn't have Bitcoin during its initial years regrets it today and nobody would like to be the one who misses out on one more Bitcoin. Everyone wants to avoid being the one who did not buy an entire dozen Bitcoin for pennies and become a multimillionaire seven years later.

There have been some custodial agencies who have taken money and then resorted to making promises that are not realistic return on investment. Confidence games usually depend on the fraudster offering promises so large that the customer becomes greedy and disregards the potential risks. Take the example of Turkish chief executive Faruk Faith Ozer. The company he runs, Thodex has run a huge, eye-catching promotion that sold Dogecoin for 75% less than market value during the cryptocurrency's rapid growth. It shouldn't come as a shock that Thodex did not have the Dogecoin, however they used people's money regardless. As of the time of writing The Turkish Central bank has outlawed the use of cryptocurrency to make payment of any kind of products or services in response.

Chapter 9: The Future Of Nfts As Well As Tokenization

The Defi & NFT

Non-fungible tokens are being embraced on the scene of decentralized financial (DeFi) area which is one of cryptocurrency's most exciting and creative areas.

Aavegotchi An experimental startup that is funded through Aave, the DeFi cash market Aave is an instance to illustrate what NFTs are being utilized in DeFi.

Aavegotchis can be described as NFT crypto-collectibles that are used in games each Aavegotchi is also equipped with Aave's tokens staking inside them as collateral. This implies that each one produces Aave yield. If the owner decides to sell their stake then the Aavegotchi disappears.

The Future of the NFTs: NFT & Blockchain

Utility tokens, cryptocurrencies, privacy tokens, security tokens... Alongside blockchain and cryptographic technology digital assets, their categories are growing and changing.

Blockchain technology is changing how we view the world of art and collectibles It's just the beginning. Tokenization is an incredible instrument with a wealth of unexplored applications.

NFTs appear to be set to last. Another issue is what NFTs can stand the test of time and keep their value. Each NFT collection is unique in its value proposition, however at the end of the day the value of NFTs is what someone will purchase them for.

If given enough time over time, the vast majority of NFTs will be useless. Certain, on the other on the other hand, will become desirable and sought-after.

Maybe your NFT may become one day the Mona Lisa! It's your only chance to know!

At present, the majority of the attention on tokens that are not fungible is on gaming, art or cryptocollectibles. The most well-known brands are increasing licensing their content for NFTs. Fantasy soccer games Sorare recently signed agreements with over 100 soccer clubs on its platform. The Smurfs and Minecraft along with Doctor Who from the BBC Doctor Who have all been issued as NFTs. In June of 2021, Twitter introduced its own collection of NFTs shortly after it announced plans to validate the authenticity of users' NFT avatars.

Non-fungible tokens can be used in games to represent items in games like skins, which allows them to be used in new games, or traded in exchange for other tokens.

However, their possibilities are more extensive; potential applications could include copyright as well as intellectual property rights. They could also be used for ticketing as well as the selling and trading of music, video games and movies.

The first feature film that was full-length which was made available as an NFT release was the thriller suspense Zero Contact in September 2021. Just a few weeks later, the thriller with a pandemic theme Lockdown was added to the mix. Autograph Tom Brady's NFT platform, introduced music as a vertical in the month of October with The Weeknd as the first signing.

Non-fungible tokens offer more possibilities to create security tokens as well as tokenizing physical and digital assets. Physical assets like real estate could be tokenized to allow share or fractional ownership. If the security tokens cannot be redeemed ownership of the actual asset can be traced as well as transparent when only tokens that represent a fraction of ownership are traded.

Non-fungible tokens can be used to verify for licenses for software, qualifications warranties, birth or death certificates. The smart contract of a non-fungible token is a permanent proof of the recipient's or owner's identity. It can also be kept in a digital wallet to facilitate acces and display. Digital wallets could someday contain evidence of each certificate, license and resource we have.

There is a difference in NFTs and Cryptocurrency

NFTs and cryptocurrencies utilize identical blockchain tech for their basis. NFT marketplaces can require customers in order to buy NFTs with cryptocurrency. Cryptocurrencies as well as NFTs however, in contrast are made and used for a variety of reasons.

The purpose of cryptocurrency is to function as currencies , storage of value, or by making it possible to buy and sell items, and crypto tokens can be fungible as are fiat currencies, like those of US dollar. NFTs create unique tokens which are used to show ownership rights and grant rights to digital products.

Popular NFTs & Case Studies

NFTs can be used to represent both digital and physical objects. The NBA is a prime example. is tokenizing videos of some of the best basketball performances throughout history, and then selling them at an income. Additionally, they receive a 5% cut of all transactions in the secondary market which is another benefit of NFTs for the creators.

The cryptopunks are tokenized pictures of 24 x 24 bit avatars that are used as tokens. There are 10,000 cryptopunks. They include 9 Aliens, 24 apes 3840 females, 88 zombies and 6,039 males each one with its own set of characteristics that differ in rarity , and are sold at an average price of $15,000.

Only 44 cryptopunks are equipped with the "beanie" feature, and they can use it immediately, increasing their value over any among the three32 cryptocurrency enthusiasts that are wearing VR goggles.

What's the importance of Non-Fungible Tokens?

There are a variety of reasons for this. Non-fungible token (NFT) is an exclusive digital asset that is able to be used to represent any digital asset on Ethereum. Ethereum blockchain, which makes it rare, measurable and worth it.

With the advent of NFTs, creators and artists are now able to use a new medium to showcase their work or collections. This has led to an era of change is setting the foundations for artists to produce and market their work and collectors are able to understand the authenticity and authenticity they purchase.

NFT assets could include digital artwork, collectors, innovative extension of music and a synergy between the three, or novel yet unexplored compositions. With NFTs, artists continue to expand the boundaries of their imagination, using NFTs in innovative and new ways.

Many people be thinking, "Can't I just screenshot the NFT without paying for it?" That's correct, however, you'll never be able to sell it at similar prices to the original. In the same way, if you were to take photos from Mona Lisa, you'd be unable to sell it. Mona Lisa, it would be difficult to locate an individual collector.

If it happens that an NFT is traded on the secondary market the new owner as well as the amount paid is immediately registered on the blockchain which is a document of transactions that cannot be altered by anyone and is available to everyone. The idea is , by making authentic certificates available online,

NFTs are able to guarantee the authenticity of the asset with the asset to which they are linked.

What you're buying is code which appears as images, and you're buying a different kind of artwork. Keep in your head that you're not purchasing the image, you're buying right to use the picture.

By design NFTs are tools artists can utilize to verify their work without the need to go through tradition's manipulations (provenance).

Because of their ability to create scarcity NFTs permit artists to decide their own prices as well as control the secondary markets they operate, which democratizes the market for artists across the globe.

Chapter 10: What Is The Best Way To Utilize Nft?

What are the games that are that are based on NFT tokens?

The games on the NFT platform could offer the players with cash prizes to take part or let players take part in the profit of the platform. Every game has to be coded in a way that it is token-compatible before it can be added to the platform. Examples of games that are currently being developed on the NFT platform include:

* StopScared (pitch of a game on a board)

* Game Fair (invest in a game company)

* STV (selling shares of the company)

NFT tokens are used to determine the amount players are compensated for playing the game, as well as to facilitate bonus transactions, such as buying game cards. The game assets can be traded with other assets, including real world currencies, in order to reflect the changes in value of the company that runs the game. Exchanges are not immediate. It could take months for one particular game item to hit their desired price before selling it at an increase in price to upgrade.

NFT Token Relay

It is expected that the NFT token relay expected to incorporate an automatic system which can immediately match any transactions sent to the relay with transactions that take place. To be effective the relay will need be able to handle high volumes of traffic as hundreds of transactions are processed within one second. The relay will be equipped with multiple cores that are able to manage multiple accounts which can each host and handle transactions as well as relay the transaction that has various transactions based on which one is the most efficient to process.

What are the rewards for NFT tokens function?

The sections below explain how the rewards transactions are split, however the fundamental procedures are the same. The procedure and structure of the rewards aren't described in this article, and it is highly recommended that attendees attend attend an NFT or NFT relay information meeting discover the method used to division of rewards.

* For startScared 1 NFT token is 0.05 USD . Bitcoin

* Game fairs 1 NFT token equals 0.01 USD. Bitcoin

*For Strava Coin 1 NFT token is 0.01 USD. Bitcoin

How and where do tokens are assigned?

The rewarded NFT tokens are distributed proportionally to the total earnings from games assets and investments. For instance, if the revenue generated from the investment amount to one million USD, the tokens are distributed to those who have made the largest investments at the close of the year. This results in an unchanging distribution for the 2019 year, based upon the 2018 revenue.

What is the best way to get tokens?

Participants must make the initial payment of 1 or three NFT tokens. When a user has made at minimum one NFT token and the system has sent the person a number of tokens when they are rewarded for their participation in the contests. The amount of tokens the participant will receive is contingent on the amount of revenue that the participant earned throughout the year. When the year those tokens can be exchanged to USD and the player can trade their tokens in exchange to purchase BTC or USD to invest in additional games offered through NFT. NFT platform.

How can my deposit tokens?

Once a user has made their first deposit, they have to pay at least 1 to 3000 NFT tokens. After the participant has deposited the tokens they need to manually input the total amount tokens they've earned from every event. Participants can only have only a limited amount of tokens that they can deposit at one time. After the user has logged into their account for the purpose of depositing their tokens they will be issued a number of tokens to participate in the contests.

What is the method of distribution of tokens to the participants?

The value of one NFT token is equal to one tenth of a US dollar BTC. Because the value of the total BTC that is mined amounts to 10,000,000 BTC equivalent to 1,000,000,000 USD, the present market value is around 1,300 USD. Based on the market cap the NFT token is worth that is 0.05 USD. But, as mentioned it is possible to trade the token at different rates , and can be worth greater or lesser in comparison to 0.05 USD. If the token is traded for 0.05 USD then the user is able to earn 0.15USD for every transaction completed in the event.

It is suggested that participants don't sell their tokens following deposits, and be patient until they receive the rewards. If participants redeem their tokens then a list of tournaments that they can participate in is made, and the participants have to deposit tokens to the list. A countdown clock will be displayed , and will continue to be counted until the tournaments are completed. When the tournament, the winners are

123

acknowledged by being awarded prizes for participation.

What is the maximum amount for reward amounts?

An unlimited amount of tokens can be used for tournaments to take part in which means that players are not able to cash out greater than 500 million coins over the year. But, players aren't bound to participate in a particular number of tournaments over the course of the year. This means that players can still receive numerous prizes. The player can receive up to 500,000 tokens in an event. If a participant earns 1000 tokens they will be able to have up to 1,500 tokens that can be used for prizes.

What are the number of tournaments scheduled?

There are a variety of tournaments scheduled throughout the year. Players are able to join to take part in any of them or select a subset of them. Players can decide to participate in tournaments where they're awarded the most tokens as well as tournaments in which they are less rewarded.

Player Bounty Program

NFT offers tournaments with prizes that players are able to win through participation in tournaments. To take part in an event, a participant must win the tournament and then spend a certain amount of tokens. The budget for tokens in an event is 5,000,000 tokens for teams with two players and 7,000,000 tokens for teams with three players. Players are awarded tokens based on the amount of tokens spent to win the tournament and also for the number of tokens that a player earns.

If players want to put the budget for tokens on a certain quantity of tokens, they may. For instance that a player wishes to put their token budget at 5,000,000 tokens they can do that and then use 3,000,000 tokens to take part in the tournament. The budget of a player's tokens cannot exceed their total number of tournament tokens. So should a participant set an amount of 5,000,000 tokens, they are not able to put their budget for tokens over 5,000,000 tokens to participate in an event.

What are the real estate properties based on? NFT tokens?

In the end blockchain technology is now making its way into the real estate market as the next wave of NFT-powered platforms is just beginning to appear that are disrupting the financial service industry with real estate loans.

OpenBazaar (OBT) is the decentralized blockchain marketplace which allows peer-to-peer trade of everything and anything comprising consumer products as well as services and everything that a decentralized market could potentially offer, announced recently they'd start an open-ended fund called the Open Bazaar Fund. The aim is to create an unstoppable cryptocurrency that is that is backed by real estate assets with the long-term aim to be run by a group of investors.

"The worth of a stable coin comes from the fact that it could be utilized for real estate deals which could be worth millions of dollars" said Alejandro De La Torre who is the general manager and executive officer of OpenBazaar. "OpenBazaar Fund is all about providing a different method to structure deals that are currently done through investments in dollars."

To utilize the token an agent in real estate can simply add it to an official document and then submit this to OpenBazaar. OpenBazaar network. Owners and owners of property are then able to make use of OBTs to purchase and sell their homes as well as funds.

The new real estate blockchain platforms and currencies provide an entirely new kind of deal. A substantial portion of investors who do not necessarily have a real stake in the property could have the opportunity to become owners, and also become involved in the real estate deal by investing.

In a discussion in a conversation with Alejandro De La Torre, OpenBazaar founder and chief designer Brian Hoffman explained that there aren't many real estate markets as large, and where "you are surrounded by millions who are buyers and seller."

"By connecting the platform with real estate-related tokens that are backed by assets, we could possibly introduce a new type of transaction in the real estate industry," Hoffman said. "It could enable people who have no interest in a specific house to purchase homes and then sell them to buyers who have an interest, but at a premium."

This is still early and, naturally the market is little overcrowded at present. In the last few weeks the blockchain-based investor network ChainFund and marketplace ChainFund created their Real Estate token, which will be used to finance purchases of residential properties, which will allow the platform to capture an amount of the 3100 billion real estate transactions which is about 50% of the world's $30 trillion economy.

Of course there is a reason why it's true that the U.S. is still the largest and the most populated real property market worldwide, and this isn't the first time that blockchain technology is used in a technology. But in order for real estate-related blockchain tokens to be successful in such a vast well-known and thriving market, it'll require more acceptance.

It doesn't take for long to appreciate the advantages of blockchain. This is a case of how the company was able develop a new market (inside an industry that is growing) by using the use of its own cryptocurrency.

"If we are successful in this endeavor, we will have a huge success in real estate investment as well as the adoption of blockchain technology," De La Torre stated. "And we'll be part of the next big wave of technological adoption."

If you're looking to learn more about a real estate token that is based on blockchain that has the possibility of creating an efficient marketplace and a more efficient system of exchange, the forthcoming ChainFund conference, scheduled for March 1-3 is the right location to attend.

How does Metauniverse work?

Metauniverse that is based on NFT tokens are a form of currency that mining companies issue following the process of mining blocks. It is used to purchase electricity as well as other mining equipment.

Certain miners mine cryptocurrency, and store some of the coins. Others make digital gold and keep a few of the coins, while others mine additional coins and keep the entire thing. Miners mine the coins through the Ethereum blockchain and then spend the money earned in cash to purchase equipment for mining, including electricity. It is called the Metauniverse. Metauniverse can be described as the cryptocurrency that is issued by miners in the aftermath of each transaction they do using the Ethereum blockchain. It's also known in the form of "fuel" which is traded in the marketplace.

How do you define Metablocks?

Metablocks is the cryptocurrency that facilitates trade in the Metauniverse. Metablocks are used as a form of currency inside the Metapanage.

What is the best way to purchase Metablocks?

Metablocks can be purchased directly using NFT tokens or bitcoin. The code in NFT tokens lets you purchase Metablocks and then sell them on cryptocurrency exchanges like EtherDelta. Metablocks are able to be purchased by using NFT tokens. Metablocks can be traded on the Bancor Network.

What is the best time to purchase Metablocks?

Metablocks are available for purchase in the beginning of each day. The token will then be made available to the market. Metablocks, however, can be bought prior to the official launch via the Bancor Network.

All Metapanage customers will receive 1 Metablocks at no cost with your very first Metapanage purchase. To purchase Metablocks later , you'll have to purchase NFT tokens.

Where can you purchase Metablocks?

Metablocks can be purchased at one of the many exchanges on Metapanage and also in your wallet or on the exchange you prefer. The code in NFT tokens allows you to purchase Metablocks, and trade them on exchanges.

How are Metaverse and NFT are they connected?

Metaverse has created an investment token that is focused on utility and liquidity. NFT allows you to trade any asset that is linked to an NFT address. They are digital assets including securities, commodities as well as financial instruments. To swap one NFT asset to another, the actual user of that asset needs to open a new account. If you decide to open an account from scratch in the first place, the person who owns the asset has to provide the asset in question and an amount to redeem. However, as of now you can trade the NFT asset in exchange for fiat currency or to any cryptocurrency you want.

So, with Metaverse, you have the option of choosing an asset that represents your capital or choose a token that is generic. It is not restricted to any specific asset, however you can utilize NFT to transfer assets such as commodities, shares FX derivatives, commodities, and any other item that is referred to by an NFT address.

NFT is able to be converted into U.S. dollars, Japanese yen, Euro, Indian rupees, Korean won, and other fiat currencies.

What are the ways Metaverse develops an eco-system of innovative products for the financial market?

With this simple application, the foundation that is the NFT is established. By expanding the ecosystem it is possible to build an ecosystem of new financial products. In reality this example allows you to establish an additional market for an NFT asset, permitting you to create a second NFT asset, which represents your stake in the NFT asset. A trusted third-party will help you to create the NFT asset, however, you can create additional NFT assets on your own If you'd like. Once you have made the asset, a buyer or seller can trade the asset in exchange for fiat money or any other cryptocurrency that they prefer. This is an addition to the asset you could sell before.

The enormous potential of the market for financial tokens

However, this isn't currently the case, NFT makes it possible to utilize blockchain technology to create a completely new class of assets. By providing assets with liquidity to this system you are able to create a new type of liquidity. The near-term future of NFT NFT is a possibility to develop an additional type of financial market that can be used for various assets. It is not necessary to create the concept of a new market structure or currency to generate worth for the financial asset. All that is required is an actual asset together with the necessary resources to enable an NFT investment to become liquid. The possibilities are endless. But a platform such as Metaverse and its extensive experience and support for developers, might be able lead the direction.

Chapter 11: Tested Strategies For Selling Your Nfts

If you simply create your NFTs and then list them on OpenSea and then, you'll generate some curiosity about the digital asset. However, we suggest to do much more than that and market your NFTs with more vigor to ensure that you increase sales more quickly. In this section we'll offer you proven strategies for effectively promoting your NFTs.

1. What makes Your NFT Unique?

You'll attract more attention for your NFT when you explain to the public why it special and distinctive. Because of their nature, NFTs are distinct, however, they will yield more results if you can help the buyer understand what makes your NFT distinct from the rest.

There's a lot of controversy currently taking place over whether it's an appropriate idea to invest into NFTs and if they are worth it. If your NFT does not seem to offer anything unique, then it's going to be much more difficult sell it. NFTs that have something special will always be viewed as the most useful. So, get your imaginative flow to write about your NFTs.

2. Utilize Twitter to promote NFTs

Instagram seems to be the ideal platform to advertise your NFTs. It is acceptable if you have more than 10k people following you on this platform. Then, you can add an NFT link on the captions of your Instagram posts.

Through Twitter you can share the NFT link within every tweet you make. Your goal is to get the attention of collectors and inform the world know that you have NFT auctions. Okay, you can create your own website that has every one of your NFT auction links and include an external link to the bio of your Instagram bio. However, it's unlikely to be as efficient as direct linking within tweets.

One of the advantages of the use of Twitter is that you're capable of sharing a variety of pictures simultaneously. When you combine compelling text with your photos, you are able to achieve the desired impact by using an array of tweets. Many artists use Twitter to promote their NFT products.

3. Utilize Other Social Media Platforms

We're not saying you shouldn't ever make use of Instagram for the purpose of displaying your NFTs. It is highly recommended to utilize this platform because it is known as a visual medium. It is similar to Pinterest.

Facebook can be another platform can be used to promote your NFTs. Anywhere you have a presence even if it is small, could be utilized to promote your NFTs. Be aware that you could expand your reach through these channels in the near future.

4. Make sure you use the Correct Hashtags

When you're posting information regarding what you are posting about on your NFT products on Facebook, you have ensure that you are using the right hashtags. Keep in mind that you will see millions social media posts that are happening simultaneously. A large portion of social media users use hashtags to search for what they're looking for.

There are investors, collectors as well as other creators on the social platforms who are searching for quality NFTs. We looked into the most frequently used hashtags on social networks to find NFTs and discovered these to include:

* #nft
* #nftart
* #nfts
* #nftartist
* #nftphotoraphy
* #nftcommunity
* #nftcollector
* #nftanimation
* #nftvideo
* #cryptoart
* #cryptoartist
* #digitalart

We recommend using these hashtags on your posts and profiles on various social media platforms.

5. Utilize Discord Forums

If you're unfamiliar with Discord it's an online social network where members can build chat rooms of their own for various reasons. Many NFT authors and collectors are currently making use of the Discord platform, and it's something you must to explore.

There are many other great options on Discord aside from the ability to create chat rooms and messaging. It is possible to store and share documents, images and other files for instance. Many cryptocurrency galleries have Chat rooms in Discord and you are able to join them so you can display your NFTs.

For certain Discord groups, you'll need an invitation from another user to join the group. There are areas on Discord where major collectors gather. Certain of them are considered to be the most famous within the realm of cryptocurrency art. If you're able to secure an invitation to these collector groups , you'll be considered an exceptional NFT artist.

6. Make an application to NFT Hunters

NFT Hunters send out a listing of the most popular NFTs to their many subscribers by email or via Telegram. Telegram messenger. They constantly search for NFT artists who have the best quality tokens in order to feature these in the weekly news.

At times, NFT Hunters will issue an "breaking breaking news" announcement to subscribers concerning an unexpected NFT trend that has been observed in the market. It's in your best interests to promote the details of your NFT collection to NFT Hunters group. It is possible to do this via email. The possibility of making sales from your NFTs is immense If you can attract the interest to NFT Hunters.

7. Advertise your NFTs Reddit

You've probably been familiar with Reddit. It's a collection of communities in which users can vote on content they enjoy. If an article on Reddit receives lots of votes, it will rank more highly on Reddit. The majority of Reddit users will view posts that have many votes.

There are subreddits dedicated specifically to the crypto arts. These are great to use together with other threads on artist communities to show off your NFTs. The most popular subreddit dedicated to crypto art has more than 8 million people. This is an enormous number of people you can't ignore.

8. Tell us about your story

A large number of NFT creators have had an impressive level of satisfaction by sharing their personal story, not just sharing their tokens. There is a chance to share this story through social media platforms along with other platforms. You can share the reason the reason you came up with a specific NFT for instance. Many collectors are keen on understanding the background story of diverse NFTs.

9. Register your NFTs on the right Marketplace

In the previous chapter, we looked at the various marketplaces available for the listing and creation of NFTs. It is crucial to pick the best platform to display your NFTs. In the event that all your NFTs are digital art of the highest quality, then OpenSea might not be the ideal marketplace to showcase your work.

Although OpenSea definitely has the highest number of users of all NFT markets (around 39 million monthly as of the present) It is also an online platform for self-service where everything can be done. It is possible that the collectors you wish to meet are hanging on Rarible for instance.

You must do your research here. Learn about the kinds of people are using the top NFT marketplaces prior to deciding where to put your tokens. Do not rely on the number of visitors to the marketplace on its own. If your NFTs target a particular market, then make use of the market in which these individuals hang out.

10. Utilize the Clubhouse Platform

Clubhouse is a relatively new social network that is audio-only which is expanding in popularity at a rapid rate. With Clubhouse users can make specific "rooms" for discussion on various subjects. Anyone who is interested in crypto art already use the platform to discuss numerous NFTs available , as well as other topics.

Join these Clubhouse rooms and ask to speak. Utilize your authority within your position in the NFT world to build followers through the site. People love to follow the experts. It will be fairly easy build your reputation in the role of an NFT expert on Clubhouse.

Another wonderful aspect of Clubhouse are the clubs. These are groups that are based on specific particular niches. There are clubs already which have been created to serve the field of NFTs. These communities are not available to join immediately, usually. Be a good listener first, and after that, someone will offer to invite you.

11. Get Started Immediately

There's never been a better time to begin making or selling NFTs than now. Make the most of the buzz around NFTs since they are a great opportunity to advertise your tokens. If you're looking to earn significant money with your NFTs, then you have to begin immediately.

There is no way to tell if the demand for NFTs will decrease drastically in the near term or whether it's staying. One thing is certain NFTs are hot in the present and the interest in the NFT market has dramatically increased in the past year. The growth continues each day.

Don't let yourself be caught out. There are thousands taking part in the NFT market each and every day. By joining right now, you stand the chance to establish your business quickly before it gets over-crowded. NFTs are still relatively new, and the demand is current. Be sure to make the most of this.

Chapter 12: What You Can Become More Involved With Nfts

After we've covered all the fascinating new ways NFTs can impact commerce and, in a broad sense our daily lives, let's discuss ways in which those who read this book can get more actively involved. Like we said it is possible for anyone to purchase NFTs. In this article, we'll go deeper into some of the top locations to purchase NFTs as well being able to sell them and then further modify them for their individual needs. Here are some excellent ways for readers to be more involved.

Best Places to Purchase NFTs

There are more than one location where one can invest in some old-fashioned NFTs. As we mentioned before, "OpenSea" is a good place to start. It's especially great for people who are trying to figure out the basics, because it is so easy and user-friendly. OpenSea claims as being an "largest NFT marketplace" and they've yet to prove incorrect on this claim. OpenSea is actually offers marketplaces within marketplaces that have an official approval of spinoff attachment platforms, such as "Decentraland." It is a decentralized platform that allows the purchase of virtual real property.

Rememberthe anticipated online real estate market where gamers are expected to buy their own part of virtual reality? This is becoming more and more popular and Decentraland could help to make that dream, if it's yours. At least, it's a virtual reality. With this one stop shop, you can purchase as as much fake, pixelated, land as you'd like.

NFT markets often target specific particular groups of investors in the same way that Decentraland caters to people seeking virtual land, the marketplace "Enjin" caters to people who want to purchase special items to play games. It's taking place. As was mentioned earlier in this book, within a few months, all sorts of virtual items purchased be able to cross over from one game or beyond all the games that are known to be used to play the game of preference.

If you're looking to take part in the exciting game-based economy, Enjin would be a excellent place to look around. What else can you purchase your amazing rune and sword, armor spaceship, spaceship, or the mysterious lama all at once? First of all, Enjin is beautifully designed as well as its design will definitely be a hit with gamers. Of course, aesthetics aren't the only thing, but what is it that Enjin actually have to provide in terms of NFTs? Everything. There is a variety of things which can be utilized in games that are popular, such as Minecraft, 9Lives Arena, Age of Rust, and other similar games.

Similar to other platforms, to buy items it is necessary to find a wallet that is compatible with Enjin. It is then necessary to purchase some Enjin Coins with which to make purchases. Once you have that, you're in good shape. Another great source to buy NFTs of all sorts is the new NFT hub--Wax.io. The site is referred to simply by the name "WAX," the good part about this site is it does not cost any transaction costs.

If you're frustrated of paying too much at other sites it might be time to try WAX. Keep in mind that WAX is not as user-friendly than sites like OpenSea. Before you use WAX you should know the basics of compatibility with regards to the protocols utilized. It is also necessary to sign up and set up an account to store your funds before using the Wax. After you've completed this and you've signed up, you'll be able to earn WAX tokens, which can be used to buy your NFTs.

Of course, it would be remiss to not refer to "Rarible" because it is now an industry standard when it relates to the purchase of NFTs. Its Rarible platform is quite simple however, it has faced many issues with fraudsters and "spam accounts" which have impacted its market. Another important thing to remember is that Rarible is primarily focused on collector's and art.

Perhaps more versatile is the platform known as "mintable" that like the name may suggest it allows users to "mint" fresh NFTs for almost everything. NFT is marketed as an "web-based" system that permits basically "anyone who has access to the internet" to create NFTs using Ethereum's blockchain.

Innovative Methods to Sell NFTs in a New Way

After we've gone over in detail the possible implications to visit market and purchase an NFT Let's look at some creative ways you can turn around and sell the NFTs at profits. If people refer to you as "Beeple," you just could be able to offer your NFT at the Chrstie's Acution House located in London, England. If you're not an Beeple person (sorry I could not resist)--then you should make an account with OpenSea!

As we've mentioned before, OpenSea is a great platform for beginners as well as experienced users. it is possible to buy and sell almost anything NFT via this flexible easy-to-use platform. If you're trying to sell something special like an unusual Tweet or text message, then you may consider the niche-specific marketplace known as "Cent."

Cent, just like OpenSea uses "Metamask." When connecting both, you are able to write any text you want. If you're looking to sell a tweet make sure to remember that when you upload it on the blockchain, it's there for the duration of time! The nature of blockchain and its indestructible state, guarantees that this part of NFT data will be encapsulated in a block and linked to the blocks that preceded it. Therefore, before you decide to tokenize your message for all time, take a moment to think about it!

What are the dangers associated with buying and selling NFTs?

We would be not truthful If we claimed that there isn't any risk involved in purchasing and selling NFTs. Each investment is subject to some risk. In reality, there is quite a bit of risk involved however, if you choose to invest prudently, you can effortlessly reduce the risk. The biggest risk when buying NFTs is the value which is associated with the specific NFT asset.

Value is dependent on the viewer and it may likely that something one considers to be a secure investment may be a shaky investment at the point it is bought. In truth, just thinking that something is valuable but that doesn't mean this is the reality. If you don't play your cards well and you don't know the best strategy, you could be left with an NFT that you've have spent a lot of money on, but that nobody else would want.

However, prior to going through the trouble of tokenizing a new NFT or buying an NFT to buy, be aware of how commercially viable that NFT could be. It's often simpler to do than it is said in a world where anything is derived from memes, tweets, and even recordings of farts (yes it's actually something that happens) are a hit in the NFT market, however other items that appear to be more sensible haven't succeeded.

In this tangled world there is no way to know what could be considered a desirable collectible item, and what could be considered to be junk or even a waste of money? This is probably the biggest danger that any person faces when they wheel and dealing with NFTs. Another issue with handling NFTs is that they're virtual. Anyone who has had to deal with cryptocurrency like Bitcoin and Ethereum is aware If you lose the password for the crypto account, it means you'll lose your Bitcoin and Ethereum that you have in your wallet --for good!

NFTs are the same because of the fact they're stored in virtual systems, it is impossible to not be certain that the platforms that host them will not eventually shut down and make your NFT unaccessible. It's not likely but the possibility present.

However there is no way to know for certain. Nothing in life is guaranteed, and even the case that you own a physical authentic Rembrandt painting in your home, the painting may just as easily be destroyed by a fire or other traumatic circumstance. In that way there are likely to be dangers the picture, but there's absolutely no reason to let the risk keep you awake at late at night, fretting about it.

Making your own NFTs -- Is worth it?
If you're artistically inclined and have a flair for drawing, you can naturally, create your own NFTs with the help of the above mentioned Rarible. Like the name might suggest, Rarible makes things rare. It is possible to take any popular digital meme or gif and transform it into an extremely rare NFT that is perfectly prepared and ready to be offered on an NFT market close to your home. To clarify almost any file with the ending JPG, GIF, PNG MP3, or TXT can be easily transformed into an NFT. People are tweeted NFT'd (how do you feel about that word?) anything from Twitters (hi Jack Dorsey!) to recipes, and memes that mock their grinning grandmother. It doesn't matter what, it could be tagged in the form of an NFT. Keep in mind what the processing cost could be. Websites such as Rarible have

what's called"gas fees" or "gas charge" that is an evocative term used to describe the processes that go through the network's complicated computing equations to "mint" an entirely new Non-Fungible Token that represents the item you are selling.

It is recommended to utilize tools like"NFT's Gas Station Tool "NFT Gas Station tool" to know what the cost of tokenization could be before you even tokenize your product. This is vital, since it's quite likely that the price charged for tokenizing an item is greater than what you would ever be able to sell it for. Therefore, at the end of the day it's the responsibility of the individual user to consider this information and then decide for themselves whether the expense of tokenization is worth it.

Repelling a few myths about NFTs

NFTs are a relatively new product which has left a lot of people in the back of the learning curve. As is often so, that gap in knowledge has prompted some myth-making to fill in the gap. However, as any two-year child is aware that just because someone claims that something is real on the internet, it does not necessarily mean that it is! In this chapter, we'll try the best we can to debunk couple of myths in relation to NFTs as well as Cryptocurrency and the blockchain.

* NFTs are valued Simply by Artificial Means

But, NFTs are just producing artificial scarcity! Since artists such as Beeple earned boku money by selling NFTs, this jolly little legend has been making rounds with great enthusiasm. It is said that NFTs create scarcity and consequently value, but they are doing it through artificial methods. Although the truth is that this could be true the sense that everything digital can be considered artificial, this statement is not true. It isn't the artificial scarcity that makes NFTs so popular and profitable, it's demand. Anything that has enough demand is definitely worth it. This isn't the same as saying NFTs can be valued "merely by manipulative methods." They are Immortal

155

I'm sorry to tell you this, Dear reader there's anything in the universe that is eternal. The very stars of the sky get born and they end up dying (wow it's almost poetic, isn't it?) and , yes, unfortunately the NFTs you have are going to expire one day too. It's true, there is a nagging issue called "Bit rot" is bound to develop and decrease the quality of the file formats. Just like fragile paintings that must be kept in good condition and repaired in art galleries across the globe, NFTs will likely need similar, but digital, care over the long term.

* NFTs will compromise the Real Art/Artists

There will always be some who will be apprehensive whenever a new method of expression is discovered. We're already hearing the complaints of those who feel that NFTs could be infringing on what they believe to be "real art" and/or "real art." Even although it's now the subject of the joke that a GIF of cats with pop tart body is being sold for millions of dollars as one of the new NTFs, it should be remembered that the quality of art and the artists who create it is always in the eyes of the observer. There aren't any elite few to determine what art is, and it's the responsibility of the general public for them to determine what it is they want. In this sense NFTs won't affect the art world in any way than any other art form that has come before it.

NFTs are destroying the environment

While it is true the power of computing that is utilized by NFTs creates a significant carbon footprint but to assert that NFTs are the main catalyst for climate change is certainly an exaggeration. Although NFTs require an enormous amount of energy to create tokens for sale, this process is not a regular thing and shouldn't be considered the main reason for climate change. As mentioned previously, there are a number of active steps being taken to reduce carbon emissions NFTs are accountable for. People in charge of Ethereum's development Ethereum have announced plans to transition from an "proof of working" format to the "proof of stake" variant, which will require less computation, which means less computing power to manage.

Chapter 13: The Working Methodology For Nfts

NFTs are crypto-tokens with a unique identity which are managed by the blockchain. This is why blockchain functions as a decentralized ledger that records the ownership and transactions of every NFT that has an identification number and code. ID and other data which no token is able to duplicate.

The creation of NFTs can be accomplished by contract-enabled blockchains, with the aid of suitable tools and assistance. Ethereum was among the first popular EOS, NEO, and currently, it has NFT standards. The tokens, as well as their smart contracts, permit to add more specific information like the identity of the owner and other personal information.

This method gives NFTs the advantages of scarcity as well as royalties, which make it appealing when combined with digital media.

Scarcity

When we talk of scarcity we state owners are the one responsible for making a decision about the amount of scarce assets they have. Take a ticket to an event of sport or concert, for instance. The person who holds the ticket determines how many tickets are sold. Similar to that the manufacturer of NFT determines the quantity of replicas to be available. This is why these replicas are available, each with slight variations.

In a different scenario the owner could only create only one NFT token, which makes it a rare highly valuable and collectible. In any event, every NFT will have its own unique identity, for instance, an identifier on any ticket or fabric that looks identical, but it isn't.

Royalties

NFTs are programmable using the software (known as smart contracts) that regulates aspects like ownership verification as well as NFT transferability. Like every software framework that incorporates a variety of functions and applications, NFTs can be configured beyond the basic concepts in terms of transferability and ownership (which can also involve connecting NFT and other assets digitally).

For instance an intelligent contract can be written. Certain NFTs automatically transfer some of the profits from each NFT sales to the owner who originally purchased it thus allowing the payment of royalty.

If someone is able to create an NFT they create the code for smart agreements that controls the property of the NFT. This code is then incorporated into the blockchain on which the NFT is managed. NFTs can be managed through various blockchains, like Ethereum (which utilizes the widely-known ERC-721 and the ERC-1155 contractual principles), Flowchain, and Wax all of which use similar procedures. There are certain NFT marketplaces, like are able to work with certain blockchains. Therefore, the particular blockchain selected for NFT could have serious consequences for the seller if the correct choices aren't made.

Distant Characteristics of NFTs What is it?

1. Incompatibility

NFTs are deemed non-interoperable since they conform to the ERC-721 standard that means that the information inside them is not utilized or shared for any purpose.

2. Rare

The total amount of NFTs worldwide is insufficient and they're scarce. They are not just scarce, but can also increase their significance. Simply put, the less the NFs they have, the more expensive they'll be.

3. It is not breakable.

The NFTs are managed and stored through Blockchain which provides them with greater security. This means that they cannot ever be destroyed, or stolen.

4. Indestructible

Non-fungible tokens cannot be exchanged for money and do not have a fixed price they aren't able to offer a fraction of the value to someone (unlike other cryptocurrency). For instance, one bitcoin is worth its weight following a move, but NFT won't.

162

5. Distinctiveness

NFTs, designed to be inspired by artwork, make use of blockchain to stand out the rest and establish the legitimacy of a piece of art. It can also help you distinguish between original objects and counterparts.

Non-fungible Tokens Benefits

Ownership Rights

In both physical and digital and physical world, the non-fungible currency could be used to identify something unique. It has been employed in the world of digital for games and collectibles (to demonstrate the owner of a certain CryptoKitty or some other item). It could also be utilized in the real world to display unique items like homes, cars as well as for craftsmanship or people. It can even be employed to restrict access to a particular area, for example, Airbnb during specific dates or to purchase tickets for flights.

The Approach to Customization

The tokens that are non-fungible, in contrast to the tokens, are able to be traded in a secure manner. The smart

163

contracts as well as fungible tokens could be able of performing certain tasks of non-fungible tokens. In the non-fungible tokens sector but the token is the sole source of information.

Additional details may be assigned to the token. These can include basic information such as names and owners. But, they can also contain information about the history of the token as well as relevant details, such as pictures of the house that the token is a representation of, prior owners of the vehicle the token is a representation of and the number of skins of characters in a game featuring similar design to what the token is associated with.

Guaranteed Trade

Transferring the ownership of digital or physical objects is usually highly risky for fraud. This is why it is difficult to accomplish or even prohibited. The exchange of information through the token is an easier and efficient process due to the security of blockchain as well as the uniqueness that non-fungible currencies offer. This means it's possible to transfer ownership of goods across different platforms or be compatible across various platforms such as games or marketplaces for NFT.

In the case of features of NFT There are a myriad of advantages. Each advantage comes with risks, and should be considered in order to prove the benefits.

The Risks Involved With NFT

Estimates

The purchase of an NFT like any other collectible one, is a risky investment because its value is increasing. Contrary to Blockchain trading cards that tokenize assets or buying physical assets NFTs are a brand new business, therefore there's no assurance that the digital asset's demand will be similar.

If there's no demand for your NFT you are buying. If that's the scenario, you'll be paying an excessive price for something that is depreciating or is not marketable. You could also set up your own NFT however there's no guarantee you'll be able to find a buyer. This could result in a loss on time and cash.

Storing things in storage

NFT sale transactions can be tracked with the blockchain system, and allows ownership to be established. Marketplaces and platforms such as Open Sea and Rarible are the places where NFTs are stored and created.

If these websites have been shut down, there's no guarantee that you'll be able to access the work. This means that it is less secure than the actual artwork on an artwork as well as game tickets as well as trading cards, which isn't likely to disappear.

The Governing

Because NFTs aren't controlled, a high degree of trust is necessary. You should be confident your eyes that the NFT you purchase is a unique piece of work or art that isn't duplicated elsewhere, or else you could be liable for an issue with copyright.

If administrators and regulators become concerned by this growing industry. In this case websites may be shut down and contributions from collectors could be reduced. This could reduce its value. NFT token in the market.

The effect of a hot Potato

It is likely that NFT games could be able to have an "hot potato" impact. Players purchase assets to sell it at an income, but the market goes down, it could be a disaster for them.

As an example, let's say that you have a game blade and wish to sell it at an amount higher than it was before. If there is a buyer it, you'll make profits; however when nobody is willing to purchase or the economy falters and you lose money, then you'll be in the red.

Chapter 14: Blockchain Solutions For Art And Collectibles

Blockchains such as Ethereum provides a variety of interesting features, including non-fungible coins (NFTs). Artists can make use of these tokens to create unique digital artwork that can be converted into physical products (such such as CryptoKitties) and even returned to the virtual world through blockchain gaming platforms such as Decentraland.

CryptoPunks are amongst the oldest kinds of cryptographic art.

Crypto Art is different from. Traditional Digital Art

Digital art is similar to Crypto Art in that it is accessible on the Internet However, their artistic methods and final products are quite different. Crypto Art is made with NFTs that are owned by one individual. In contrast the digital art can be reproduced for a long time -- usually without the authorization of the creator. Due to its location on a server.

Digital art is often of little value other than its commercial usage. However the crypto market, such as cryptokitties can be an investment that could yield huge profits for first-time buyers in auctions or swap meet. But, it's unclear whether these gains will be enough to pay for the cost for the purchase cost.

"Art is always an expression of society's present state".

It's a fact that art has been around throughout the centuries, even though the definition of art has changed over the years. It is also evident that there are many ways to categorize art and the way it is displayed as art that can be hung on the walls, as digital art' which is sold or uploaded to computers, as physical sculptures, or live performances.

It's a kind of digital art that works by mathematical concepts. It's been used to secure sensitive information over time, but it's now a growing field of study with a variety of practical applications, from protecting credit card information to running massive worldwide computing platforms. The kind of encryption that we're concerned with here is the one that generates "non-fungible tokens" (NFTs) on blockchains, not the type that protects our personal information.

As NFTs have gained popularity and recognition, they've had the opportunity to make truly distinctive artworks that don't just represent them, but also carry financial value.

It's not meant to mean conventional digital art isn't a thing, but it does have distinct characteristics. NFTs, on the contrary side, are more intimate and beneficial for the "creator because they may be scarce, but yet be available to everyone.

"Non-fungible tokens (NFTs) are among blockchain's most exciting developments." They're referred to as "non-fungible" since each token is unique and is exactly like the real world goods which cannot be exchanged or replaced with similar items. For instance, you can make use of your funds to purchase an art work that is tangible. However, it will have nothing more than the money you spent to purchase it. If you purchase an ERC721 token on the blockchain using the same amount of money that you have, you will effectively "own" an internationally unique artwork.

It is vital to understand that tokens are not cryptocurrency in and of themselves They represent digitally the value of an asset or service on the blockchain. We've all heard about cryptocurrencies such as Bitcoin and NFTs, however NFTs are a unique invention to represent 'tokens' each one is unique and has metadata about it. These "tokens" can range from digital kittens to images and everything else that's been digitalized! The concept doesn't have to be related to money, either.

In the conventional economy there are similar concepts to holding something other than usual asset classes such as securities (stocks) or cash and commodities (like oil or gold). Collectibles (such as baseball and toys) cards) as well as antiques (fine art) each have a certain amount of value added due to their rareness. However. NFTs take this concept further since every piece is unique and can't be replaced with another similar piece. That means anyone has the right to own a digitally unique artwork that is more than an enhancement to your portfolio of investments. It can be a physical item in your day-to-day life. You can make it a part of your home, swap it to purchase something else, trade it for something else, or make use of its worth in games or digital media.

Chapter 15: The Nft Boom

As we've discussed in previous chapters the NFTs we have discussed are assets in digital form that are not fungible or transferable. They can also be traded. They can represent nearly everything from physical assets to games and even celebrities.

This is the final category which has been the subject of the current interest in NFTs. Blockchain technology has enabled an increase in the number of cryptocurrency assets that can be traded peer-to peer and do not need an entity that is centrally controlled like a corporation or government to confirm their authenticity.

As we've discussed in the previous chapters the issue has huge implications for both governments and businesses that are trying to simplify their operations and reduce overhead costs. But what is the case for the average citizen?

The recent surge in blockchain-based collectibles especially those based on the Ethereum blockchain, has resulted in an entirely new type of asset that is held by anyone around the world, and is known as Crypto Collectibles.

Although this might sound appealing to many but there's some confusion over what exactly a cryptocurrency collectible is and what it is different in comparison to other cryptocurrency assets, such as cryptos.

Are there bubbles in the market for NFTs?

If we go back to the fundamentals of an economic bubble, it is evident that there has been an extreme rise in the price in non-fungible coins. But what is the length of time the bubble continue to last? It's a question only time will be able to answer. It's possible that NFTs may be in the midst of a bubble, and the bubble could pop however we will not know whether it is true until the market has adjusted to the new price.

I'm not trying be a gloomy sage however there are some indicators which may indicate there is a possibility that there is a possibility that the NFT market may be in the midst of a state of bubble. The cryptocurrency market is known for its volatility, and there are instances that things appear to get out of hand. We've seen the cryptocurrency market go through some of these crashes although they may be difficult for some, it's important to keep in mind that many such markets have been able to recover. It's probable for it is possible that the NFT market will rebound also.

What's driving the current surge in NFTs?

1. The speculation

The market for cryptocurrency is awash with speculators and people who believe they are able to forecast the future. People have been buying NFTs hoping that their value will increase. This isn't necessarily bad however, it can cause some uncertainty. If the market fluctuates and people suffer, some are injured and some earn profit. The aim is to earn money, however many can't know how high or low the price could go.

2. Media Attention

A lot of the top NFTs are used in virtual worlds and games. There are a few crypto art projects becoming popular in social media and in the. When something receives this kind of attention, it's not difficult for investors to hop onto the bandwagon and purchase NFTs at a higher cost. If there is a greater demand for NFTs then the cost will rise.

3. Limited Supply

There is a limit to the amount of NFTs which are being developed every year to support each particular project. The number of tokens available can be purchased at any moment is decreasing due to the projects creating new tokens. Some think that this decrease in supply will result in the price to be higher, but this isn't always the case. The higher price can only happen if there's greater interest in the coins.

4. The growing the popularity of games that are decentralized and virtual worlds

The popularity of games that are decentralized as well as virtual reality is growing. There are a variety of initiatives that are developing new game and virtual environments that make use of NFTs.

Some of these have had success, while others have not been successful. When a project fails it could be a sign that it is likely that the worth of NFTs that are associated to that project could decrease.

What is the future of NFT?

The future of tokens that are non-fungible is uncertain. The current value isn't long-term The market itself is priced too high however it doesn't mean there won't be a revival. There are many people who believe in the potential that is NFTs or crypto-art, and it is possible that there will be an upswing within the next few years. We'll have to wait and observe whether the price of the cryptocurrency will rise or fall over the coming months or even years.

Let's look at the most sought-after NFT category of collectibles.

Crypto Art

The most sought-after collection in cryptocollectibles are art. As we've covered in previous chapters early digital assets based on blockchain were mostly digital files like videos or music. But one issue with this was that they could easily be copied and shared, without having a central authority to prove its authenticity.

The solution to this issue came in the form Crypto Art. By putting an artwork on the blockchain, artwork on the blockchain, you can guarantee that there is only one copy of the artwork and no one is able to duplicate this without breaking encryption. Artists are able to sell digital copies of their work and ensure that no one else will be able print copies or offer them for sale.

The result is numerous businesses popping up offering digital versions of artworks at different costs. But they're not the only ones selling this kind of product. Numerous other kinds of businesses have started selling NFTs that represent physical objects like clothes or vehicles and go so far as to offer digital assets that are tangible assets like the building of a business or home!

Although this might sound appealing, there are limitations on what you can accomplish using these funds. In particular, you are not able to directly transfer the ownership rights of an asset which the NFT is a representation of. This means you can't sell your home or the car that you own, but you could sell the NFT in exchange for it.

The same is true for crypto art too. Although you are technically able to purchase the digital version of an artwork, you are unable to actually buy the artwork. To do this, you'll need to purchase the physical artwork and verify its authenticity by using an online platform that is based on blockchain, like The Ascribe Platform or the Proof of Existence.

As a result, numerous companies have developed NFTs that represent assets they don't actually own , and are , therefore, digital representations of the assets. This can be difficult for those who aren't familiar with blockchain technology. It can be difficult to discern between businesses which are actually selling physical assets and those who sell digital representations of the assets.

Let's look at some of the various forms of crypto art

Crypto Collectibles:

Although Crypto Art is popular among blockchain enthusiasts, many who aren't in the cryptocurrency world may not have heard of it until now. This is why a lot of collectors of crypto have made the decision to take their hobby one step further and develop blockchain-based digital assets which represent the real world items.

To accomplish this, you must be able to program smart contracts using Ethereum. Ethereum blockchain. This is why there are many businesses that have emerged that offer services to create crypto collectibles like CryptoKitties as well as Etheremon.

The major difference between NFTs with crypto art and NFTs is, with these collectibles, you are able to take ownership over the value that an NFT symbolizes. This means that you could purchase the CryptoKitty by borrowing it from somebody else, and later transfer ownership to another person who will pay you for it. You could also trade in an Etheremon or other cryptocurrency collectible through an exchange, such as OpenSea or RareBits to exchange it for cryptocurrency.

As we've discussed in the previous chapters in previous chapters, this is among the most appealing aspect of Blockchain technology since blockchain technology allows us to develop new types of assets that would not have been possible prior to now. But, there are some limitations associated with these types of assets too:

There aren't any laws yet in force concerning how to use NFTs as well as crypto-collectibles, in general, therefore there could be risk associated with purchasing NFTs.

There's an abundance of uncertainty regarding how legal these investments. A lot of countries haven't yet come up with laws that allow the use of crypto collectibles , also known as NFTs, and there aren't any laws that ensure that you are protected if someone sells you a crypto collectible that was fake , or even if it was taken from someone else.

There's also a dearth of information about these assets and their functions. As we've discussed in earlier chapters, there are many who don't comprehend how blockchain technology operates and what it is that makes it different from fiat currencies that are traditional. It can be difficult for them to know what they're buying when they buy a cryptocurrency collectible, also known as NFT.

The result is that a lot of people interested in purchasing NFTs and crypto collectibles aren't sure of what they should buy or where to purchase the items from, so there isn't much innovation in this sector in comparison to other kinds of crypto assets, such as crypto currencies.

However, this doesn't suggest that the future of these types of assets looks negative. There's plenty of opportunity for these assets , as we'll see in the following:

Virtual Reality:

Conclusion

NFTs have a virtually limitless number of possibilities and opportunities, and recently record-breaking sales has helped the growth of the technology. One of the major obstacles to widespread adoption is the inadequacy of knowledge about the blockchain and cryptocurrency technology in the general population. Development of Your Base founder John G Fields said, "If you teach people how to taste it and allow them to experience it, they won't be overwhelmed by the technology." Since new users of the Blockchain sector have to be aware of the importance of safeguarding their private keys and wallets to ensure that hackers are not able to gain access to their Digital assets, protection is an integral element in this course of instruction. Many digital collections, relics and investments, that could be destroyed are distinctive due to the exclusivity and rarity of the items they hold. To protect their integrity, creators and artists should ensure that complete rights to copyright and licensing are contained in intelligent contracts. The majority of cryptocurrency wallets available are extremely complex and difficult to use, particularly for those who are new to the technology and users who are new to the field. Just to name a few examples, wallets like Coinbase Wallet, Pillar Wallet, Enjin Wallet, or WAX Wallet (WCW) are constantly being developed and released to address this issue as seen below. NGRAVE ZERO is another wallet worth keeping an eye on since it's one of the "coldest" and safest cryptocurrency wallet on the market. It's also extremely user-friendly and simple to use which makes it a great option for those who are new to. It's interesting to consider that ZERO's top-quality tactile display is not just an environment that is secure and safe that allows users to store and trade their virtual property and assets, but also the ability to let owners to show their virtual collection and other assets to anyone else by using a tiny handheld device.

184